Woodcarving
A Foundation Course

Woodcarving
A Foundation Course

Zoë Gertner

Guild of Master Craftsman Publications Ltd

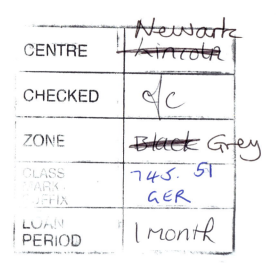
UNIVERSITY OF LINCOLN

First published 1997 by
Guild of Master Craftsman Publications Ltd
166 High Street, Lewes,
East Sussex BN7 1XU

Reprinted 1998

© Zoë Gertner 1997

Photographs by Helen Perry

Drawings by John Yates

Cover photograph by Dennis Bunn

ISBN 1 86108 059 X

Designed by Fineline Studios

Set in New Aster and Akzidenz Grotesk

Origination in Singapore by Master Image

Printed and bound in Singapore under the
supervision of M.R.M. Graphics.

Contents

About the author

Zoë Gertner specializes in teaching woodcarving, and is a fully qualified teacher, having studied anatomy and kinesiology as part of her degree. She teaches students of all ages, from eight years upwards, from all walks of life, including the inmates of one of Her Majesty's prisons. Zoë has been a professional woodcarver since 1980, and undertakes frequent commissions. She lives and works in Somerset, and her carvings can be found in local churches there as well as in private collections all over the world.

Part 1
Preparation

Chapter 1

About Wood

The nature and structure of wood

Successful carvings always utilize and exploit the natural characteristics of the wood from which they are made, carved in sympathy with the materials' inherent properties, never in spite of them. Therefore, it is very important to have an understanding of the way in which wood grows and its resulting structure.

Wood is divided into two specific types: hardwood and softwood. However, these terms do not refer to the actual hardness of the wood, but to the botanical classification of trees, which are divided into two groups: hardwoods and softwoods. Hardwood trees are deciduous, having broad leaves that are shed in winter; softwoods are the coniferous trees, having mainly needle-like leaves and remaining evergreen. They have a less complex cell structure from hardwoods, as shown in Fig 1.1.

On the whole, hardwoods are more durable, and more of them are suitable for carving. However, some softwoods, such as yew, can be a delight to carve. (You will find a glossary of woods suitable for carving on page 175.)

All woods are made up of fibres that lie roughly parallel to each other (see Fig 1.2). If you look along a length of, say, mahogany, you will be able to see them as tiny stripes. This part of the wood is known as the long grain. If

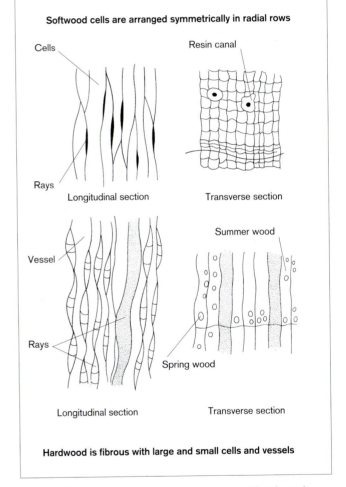

Fig 1.1 The cellular structures of softwood and hardwood.

you look at the end of the piece, where the fibres have been cut crossways, you will be able to see them as rough specks. This area is known as the end grain. Mahogany is a good wood to examine for these features, as it is coarse-grained.

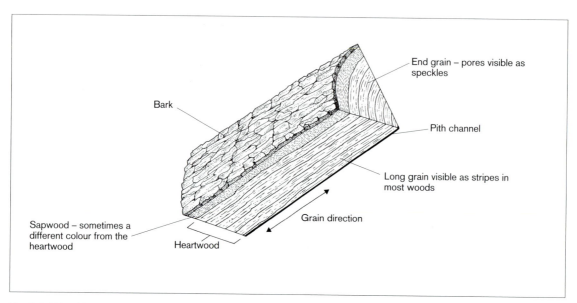

Fig 1.2 Wood is made up of fibres that lie roughly parallel to each other and which can be seen as stripes when the wood is split lengthways. These are known as the long grain. If the wood is sawn across the grain, the ends of the fibres (the end grain) can be seen.

Fig 1.3 A close-grained wood has tightly-packed fibres in which the tiny pores of the end grain are often invisible. The wood is dense and heavy for its size. Usually only small pieces are available because it is slow growing. It is ideal for intricate carvings. Typical examples are holly, yew, lignum vitae and box. A coarse-grained wood has loosely-packed fibres with large open pores in the end grain. Mostly, it is soft and easily carved, but it is not suitable for finely-detailed carvings. Typical examples are ash, ailanthus and oak.

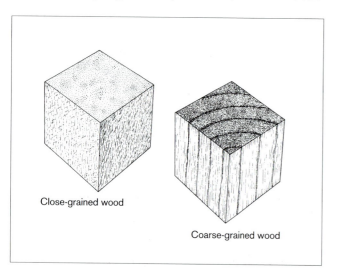

In general, coarse-grained woods are used for large, bold and possibly tooled carvings, whereas close-grained woods are suitable for small detailed carvings (see Fig 1.3).

Always carve with the grain or across it (which is harder), but *never* against it, as shown in Fig 1.4. If you do this, your tool will dig into the wood, ripping and tearing it. Any cuts you do achieve will be dull. If you find yourself cutting against the grain, always stop, turn the work around or change your own position, and cut in the opposite direction.

Within each tree (whether hard or softwood), there are two main types of wood: the sapwood, which lies just beneath the bark, and the heartwood, which lies beneath the sapwood (see Fig 1.5). Sapwood is usually easier to cut, but is also more susceptible to woodworm. If you cut across a section of a log, you will be able to see the concentric rings of growth, one for each year of the tree's life. Sometimes, the rings are wider on one side than the other, due to growing conditions on that side being more favourable, or the tree leaning to one side during growth.

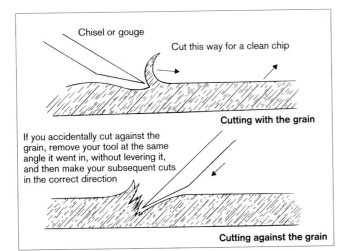

Fig 1.4 Always cut with the grain, never against it. If the freshly cut surface is dull and ragged, you are cutting in the wrong direction; it should be clean and shiny. Cutting against the grain will tear the wood and may even split it.

Fig 1.5 Sapwood lies beneath the bark of a tree, and the heartwood below that. The former is easier to cut, but is more susceptible to attack by woodworm. When you cut across a log, the concentric growth rings will be seen, one for each year of the tree's life.

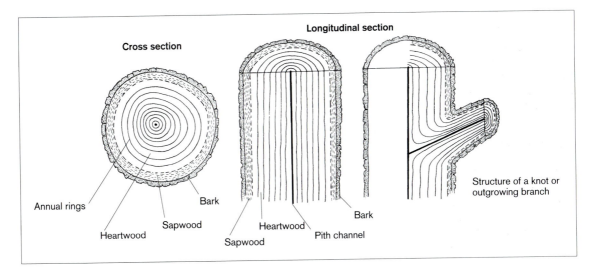

Choosing the correct wood for your project

It will be useful to bear in mind the following when selecting wood for a project:

- How large will the finished piece be?
- Is weight a factor? Will the carving need to be lifted or posted?
- How much time do you have to complete the project? Can you wait for exactly the right wood to come along, or do you have a deadline to meet? Remember that hard woods, such as yew, oak, ash or elm, take much longer to carve than soft woods such as lime.
- Which will be more suitable: a light wood or a dark wood? Always avoid staining a light wood; choose a dark wood to begin with. Remember that the eventual location of the piece will influence this decision; a light carving will show up nicely against a dark

background, and vice versa.

- If the piece is to have narrow unsupported areas, such as outstretched arms, the grain must run along them, not across them, otherwise they will break off easily. Does the grain pattern allow for this? If it does not, can the design be modified so that the projecting part can be supported at some point along its length or at its end, using the cross grain?

- Look out for strong figuring, such as grain patterns, knots and so on, which must either be incorporated into the design of your piece or avoided.

- What kind of surface texture do you require: smooth and polished (choose a close-grained wood) or rugged and tooled (use an open-grained wood)?

- What is the texture of the wood like? If it is *too* coarse, it will probably crumble if you attempt any fine carving.

Avoid using woods that have an interlocked grain. This will be visible as adjacent stripes running in opposite directions as a result of the wood growing spirally (see Fig 1.6), or flecked stripes running at angles. Whichever way you cut, you are likely to cut into fibres running the opposite way, so that you constantly have to change the direction in which you work to obtain clean cuts.

Always consider the pattern that the grain makes on the surface of the wood. A highly-figured grain pattern might be ideal for a bold, smooth sculpture, but may detract from, for example, a detailed piece in the round, by giving an unintentional sneer to a figure's face, or distracting from the subject of a relief panel.

Obtaining wood
Sources of supply

You can obtain wood from a wide range of sources, from fallen trees to timber merchants, and once friends learn that you carve, you will often receive offers of wood that they no longer require. If you are lucky enough to be able to (legally) collect your own supply, remember that it will probably need to be stored and seasoned (see page 7).

What to look for

Always examine a prospective purchase with great care. There is no such thing as a perfect piece of wood, but there are signs to look out for and avoid at all costs. Look closely at the ends, where there may be cracks that can extend deep into the wood, making it unusable. Choose a piece that is reasonably

Fig 1.6 Where possible, avoid using wood with interlocked grain, which is difficult to carve, because it will mean frequently having to change the direction in which you cut.

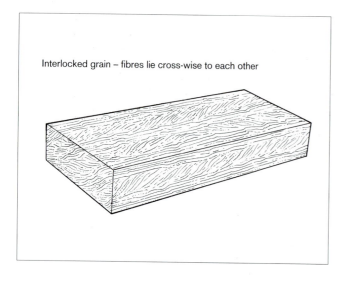

Interlocked grain – fibres lie cross-wise to each other

(or completely) knot free, straight-grained, with a firm texture. A 'woolly' texture indicates rot, and such wood will not cut cleanly.

Look for any evidence of decay, often indicated by a musty smell. Not all decayed wood is useless, but it is best avoided for any of your first carving projects. Always avoid wood with worm infestation.

If your intended project is a relief carving, use a flat unwarped piece with a straight grain, free from knots and bruises. Avoid the very ends of planks as well, since these are often marked with paint for identification, which can mask damage and may penetrate the wood for some way.

Other flaws to look for

See Fig 1.7. Cracks and splits in the wood are called shakes, and occur when adjacent layers of fibres separate. There are several common types.

Star and heart shakes

These radiate from the centre of the log and can be deep and wide. They are caused by shrinkage through old age, or by too rapid drying.

Ring and cup shakes

These are gaps between the concentric growth layers, and can be deep. They are caused by poor growing conditions or by lack of nutrition during growth.

Checks

These are fine longitudinal cracks on the perimeter ends of a log, caused by the wood losing moisture too quickly. They do not extend across the whole of the cross section, and are usually fairly short in length, so that if the affected ends are removed, there may be a sound and usable length of wood left over.

Fig 1.7 You may come across a variety of flaws in logs. Common among them are checks, heart and star shakes, and ring or cup shakes. Checks will be visible as small cracks on the end of a log and can be removed by sawing off the affected wood. Heart and star shakes can often be deep, emanating from the pith in the centre. Either split the log along its widest crack or cut off the affected portion. Ring or cup shakes occur where the annual rings have separated. Sometimes the entire core drops out, leaving a usable ring of wood. Here you can see, from left to right: rot in the centre of a log, star and radial shakes, and ring or cup shakes.

Coping with flaws

Flaws in wood are so common that often you will be forced to either cut them out or use a different piece of the same wood, or modify your design to take account of them. Concealment is another option. For example, if the wood contains a small crack, you may be able to run the edge of some detail along it or re-arrange the layout of decorative features, such as leaves or stems, so that one edge runs along the crack. Alternatively, it may be possible to shape such a feature into the crack to make use of it, rather than mask it completely.

Cracks can also be filled. The wax polish used in the finishing process often achieves this on its own, but for larger cracks you may need to use coloured wax crayons (wax sticks), which are specially made for this purpose. To obtain the correct colour match, pare off a little of the most suitably coloured crayon into the bowl of an old teaspoon and melt it using a warm waterbath. Never apply direct heat – it will cause the wax to ignite. Then add other colours until you obtain a good match. Use a knife blade to press the molten wax into the crack and allow it to set, scraping the excess from the adjacent surface. If the colour is still not correct, scrape it out with the knife tip and start again.

Alternatively, you can use glue and fine sawdust (taken from the waste wood of your carving), mixing this into a thick paste. Press the paste well down into the crack and leave overnight to set. Then remove any excess with a scraper as part of the usual finishing process.

Very wide cracks can be filled using slivers taken from the waste wood, as shown in Fig 1.8. Cut the slivers so that the grain of each runs in

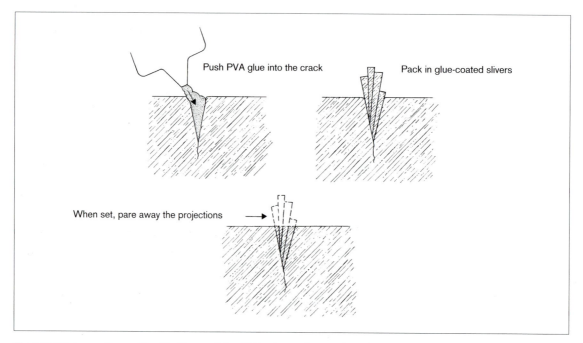

Push PVA glue into the crack

Pack in glue-coated slivers

When set, pare away the projections

Fig 1.8 Wide cracks can be filled by applying PVA glue to the crack and packing glue-covered slivers of wood tightly into it. The slivers should be cut from the waste wood of the carving and their grain should run in the same direction as the wood surrounding the crack. When the glue has set, pare the tops of the slivers off.

the same direction as the wood surrounding the crack. Press some glue into the gap and pack the glue-covered slivers in as closely and tightly as you can. Leave the tops proud of the surface, and pare them away once the glue has set.

Occasionally, cracks may appear in the wood while you are working on it, particularly during particularly hot weather. To prevent this, keep the wood wrapped in a damp cloth or towel, or Clingfilm when you are not working on it. Alternatively, collect the chips carved from the piece, moisten them slightly and keep them with the carving in a polythene bag between carving sessions. As the carving nears completion, remove it from the bag for increasing periods of time so that it dries gradually.

The stresses that occur in a log as it dries can be relieved by drilling a series of holes in the base that extend deep inside. Keep the holes away from the edges, and bear in mind the shape of your carving. When the carving is complete, the holes can be plugged. This is also a useful way of reducing the weight of a large carving.

Knots that cannot be incorporated into the design of the carving can be removed and the holes plugged. Bore out each knot with a drill bit that is slightly larger than the flaw (if possible). Then mark a piece of wood with the grain running in the corresponding direction to the main piece (vital if the repair is not to look amateurish) with the drill bit to obtain the correct plug size. Use callipers for large knots. Cut out the plug carefully, using a fine-toothed saw followed by a gouge or chisels and then a scraper to shape it accurately, and glue it into place. Leave overnight, then pare it down with a plane, chisel or scraper.

Always keep logs that have outgrowing branches or roots. You may find that their shapes will be ideal for projects in the future. A good example is the project in Chapter 12.

Very hard woods, such as walnut and yew, can be slow and tiresome to carve, but they can be softened by wrapping them in a damp cloth when not being worked on. Alternatively, your carving can be left out in the rain or in a bucket of water; it will come to no harm. Walnut can also be sticky to carve, as can elm, but scrubbing the area about to be carved with lukewarm water will make it much easier.

Very soft woods can also be difficult to carve, being fluffy and woolly. Regrinding the tool bevel to a larger and shallower angle will help. The wood can be hardened, however, by applying a mixture of shellac and surgical spirit, or a proprietary sanding sealer. Alternatively, PVA glue can be rubbed into the surface with your fingers, or a solution of cascamite glue brushed on.

Storing and seasoning your wood

Collecting and storing your own carving wood will ensure that you have a ready supply without having to rely on timber merchants, and it is always nice to know where a particular piece came from. Ideally, cut your wood into sections about 12in (30cm) long, which should leave enough to carve if you have to cut off the ends because of cracks.

Recently-felled wood will contain a lot of

moisture, and if the wood is allowed to dry too quickly, it will crack badly. If possible, arrange for a tree to be felled in the autumn, when the sap will have fallen, as it will contain less moisture than one cut in the spring. Store the wood in a cool airy place, under cover. Since most moisture will be lost from the ends of the logs, coat them with candlewax, car underseal or polyurethane, which is colourless. This will slow down the rate of moisture loss.

It is well worth trying to season logs in their natural form, since they will offer you greater flexibility in the shape of your carving and are likely to have symmetrical grain patterns. Stack logs with gaps between them so that the air can circulate around them easily, as shown in Fig 1.9. Sycamore and lime should be stored vertically, otherwise it will become discoloured. Inspect your wood frequently, and if any logs show signs of cracking badly, you will have to split them along the deepest crack to relieve the internal stresses.

Be particularly vigilant during hot weather. If necessary, you can cover the logs with polythene sheeting, which will slow down the rate of drying. You can also sprinkle water over the logs, but do so sparingly, otherwise the wood will become smelly.

If you do need to split a log because of cracking, stand it on a firm surface and make a shallow groove with an axe and hammer from the crack to the other side of the log. Then place the axe blade in this groove, over the pith, with its handle above the crack. Gently tap the head of the axe with the hammer until you hear a cracking sound as the wood splits. It may be necessary to open up the gap with wedges. If the two sections of the log do not separate cleanly, this will be because the wood has a wind or twist in it. Simply cut through the offending portion with a saw or chisel, resisting the temptation to pull the two halves apart, as this may damage the wood and render it useless.

If the log you want to split contains protruding knots or branches, you must cleave it at right angles to the largest of these, regardless of where the main crack is situated. If you do not, you will end up with a twisted, useless piece of wood, possibly with the axe jammed firmly in it.

Remember that wood is hygroscopic, that is it will absorb and release moisture according to the condition of the air that surrounds it. It should not be exposed to extreme temperature fluctuations.

Fig 1.9 Store logs with gaps between them so that air can circulate. Some, such as lime and sycamore, should be stored upright to prevent discolouration. Planks for relief carvings should be stored off the ground with spacers between them.

Chapter 2

Tools, Materials & Equipment

Two of the commonest questions I am asked by aspiring woodcarvers are: 'What tools should I buy?' and 'Where can I buy them?' There is such a wide and confusing choice that it is easy to buy tools that are unsuitable, which can be a very expensive mistake. I base my teaching on hand tools only, since very few of my students own or want to invest in bandsaws and other power tools, and I want them to be able to continue their carving after they leave.

All kinds of woodcarving tools are available. Some are of excellent quality, others are of poor or indifferent make; while old used tools can also be found and may be of use. This chapter will help you choose the tools you need, showing you what to look for and what to avoid.

Choosing your first carving tools

Woodcarving tools can be classified as either gouges or chisels, the former being used most frequently. Some of the tools will have curved or bent blades (see Fig 2.1), and all can range

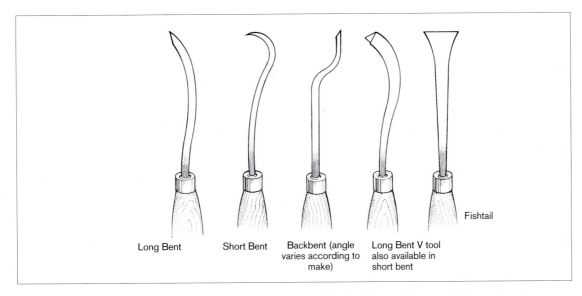

Long Bent Short Bent Backbent (angle varies according to make) Long Bent V tool also available in short bent Fishtail

Fig 2.1 Both gouges and chisels may have straight or curved blades. Those with straight blades (London pattern) will be of most use (see Fig 2.3); never use a mallet with a curved blade, as the tool may break.

in width from less than ⅟₁₆in (2mm) to more than 2in (50mm). A gouge always has a curved cutting edge, or sweep, regardless of blade size and shape, while the cutting edge of a chisel is always straight (see Figs 2.2 and 2.3).

A carver's chisel has a bevel on each side of the cutting edge, while a carpenter's chisel has just one. A carver's gouge has only one bevel, on the outer cutting edge, not the inside. The curvature of the blade prevents the corners of the cutting edge from digging into the wood. If a straight chisel is used, its corners will tend to sink in, scoring the surface and leaving unsightly ridges and splits in the wood (see Fig 2.4). These straight chisels are used for lettering, chip carving, and cutting along the borders of relief work.

Some gouges have a very shallow curve, or sweep, to the cutting edge and may be difficult to distinguish from a chisel. Look carefully end on to the cutting edge: if there is the slightest suggestion

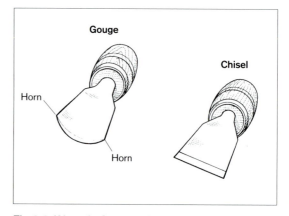

Fig 2.2 (Above) Gouges always have curved cutting edges, while chisels have straight edges.

Fig 2.3 (Below) The most versatile carving gouge is the London pattern, which has a straight blade and can be used by hand or with a mallet. The cutting edge has a bevel on the underside.

Fig 2.4 (Bottom) Because a gouge has a curved cutting edge, the corners (or horns) can be kept above the surface being worked, producing a clean cut. If you try to use a chisel to remove chips, it will dig in and damage the surface.

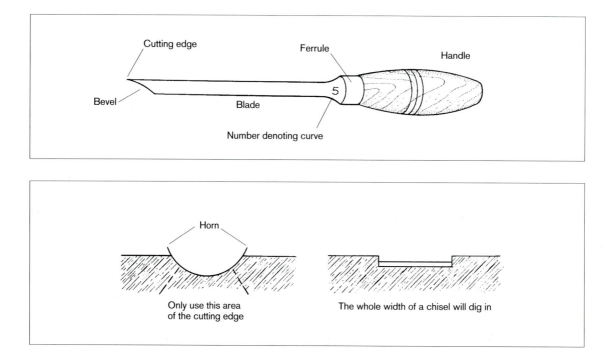

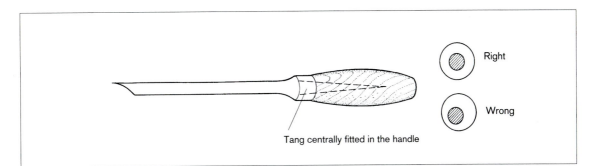

Right

Wrong

Tang centrally fitted in the handle

Fig 2.5 When buying carving tools, make sure that the blade is fitted centrally in the handle, otherwise the latter will split when used with a mallet. The gouge will also be difficult to control.

of a curve, you have a gouge in your hand. It is important to know the difference between the two, as they are sharpened differently and can easily be spoiled if the wrong technique is used. A gouge will usually have a number from 2 or 3 upwards stamped on the shank near the handle, representing its curvature.

What to look for when buying carving tools

It is best to buy tools with handles already fitted to them, so that you can start carving as soon as possible. However, if you have access to a lathe and are skilled at using it, you can buy tools without handles and turn your own. The handle should be sound and comfortable to hold, with the grain of the wood running along its length, in line with the blade. Some makes of tool have handles with ferrules, and these should be smooth, without any sharp edges. Check that the blade is fitted centrally in the ferrule and is in line with the handle (see Fig 2.5), otherwise eventually the handle will

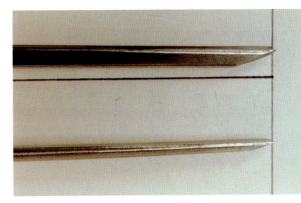

Fig 2.6 A gouge that is thicker in section than width (top) will be heavy and difficult to use for delicate work, especially in confined spaces. It also needs a very long bevel to cut properly and is best avoided. A thinner-sectioned gouge (bottom) is preferable.

split due to repeated mallet blows. You may also have difficulty in controlling your cuts, or not be able to cut at all.

Examine the cutting edge carefully and reject the tool if it is blued, pitted or damaged in any way. Check the quality of the steel: it should not be pitted or scored, but smooth and shiny. The blade of a good quality tool should have rounded edges all down its length, otherwise you will develop blisters and callouses on your fingers when carrying out delicate hand carving. Look along the blade from the side: your tool will be cumbersome and unbalanced if it is thicker in section than in width (see Fig 2.6). Do not worry about it

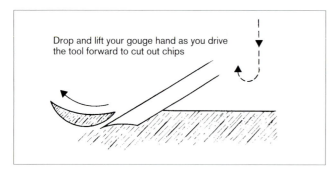

Fig 2.7 A gouge removes chips with a scooping action.

Fig 2.8 Gouges usually have a number stamped on the blade, close to the handle (also shown in Fig 2.3). The higher the number, the greater the curvature of the blade and the deeper the cut.

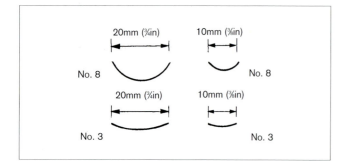

Fig 2.9 Gouges are specified by width (from horn to horn) and curvature. Regardless of width, the gouge number always refers to the same curvature.

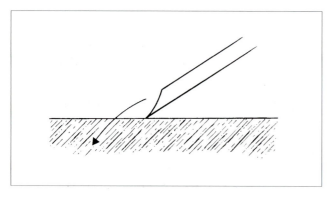

Fig 2.10 A gouge with a bevel on the inside of the cutting edge will tend to dig into the wood, rather than scoop out chips, so it would not be suitable for carving.

breaking, since this is only likely to occur if you abuse the tool by using it as a lever.

As a general rule, it is not worth buying a set of carving tools, as it will probably contain several that will be of no use to you, so you would be wasting your money. Buy only one or two gouges to start with, then build up your collection as you need them. As with any tools, you will get what you pay for, so buy the best you can afford.

Gouges

As its name suggests, a gouge removes chips of wood with a gouging, or scooping, action (see Fig 2.7). The sweep of the cutting edge can range from a shallow arc to a deep U-shape, and various widths are available. The sweep is referred to by a number, which is usually stamped on the back of the blade, close to the ferrule. The higher the number, the greater the curvature and deeper the chip, regardless of the width of the tool, as shown in Fig 2.8. Thus, while a ¼in (6mm) no. 3 will be narrower than a ¾in (18mm) no. 3, it will have the same amount of curvature (see Fig 2.9).

Turn a gouge over and you will see the bevel where the cutting edge slopes towards the tip of the blade. The length and angle of the bevel affects the way in which the tool cuts, and how easy it is to use. The bevel should be bright and shiny to minimize friction when cutting. If you touch the edge of the blade after using it, you will be surprised at how hot it becomes through friction. Do not buy a gouge with a bevel on the inside of the cutting edge, as this will oppose the scooping action of the blade, making it impossible to control your cut, as shown in Fig 2.10.

The bevel should be slightly hollowed across its width, otherwise it will act like a wedge in the wood, and the tool will not cut easily. It will wear with use, becoming shorter and thicker, which will make the tool more and more difficult to handle, until eventually it must be re-ground to restore the correct cutting angle. However, this will normally occur over a considerable period of time.

The best angle for the bevel is 27°. Some carvers advocate a greater angle for particularly hard woods, but I have never found that this makes any significant difference. However, when carving softer woods, such as pine, I have discovered that the bevel needs to be longer and shallower, otherwise the softer parts of the grain tend to tear, although the resinous harder areas may be cut cleanly. This is particularly important when carving lettering; you will find that you have to re-grind your bevelled chisels to obtain a clean cut if you are carving an inscription in soft wood.

In my opinion, the best woodcarving gouges are made by the Swiss firm Pfeil and I recommend that you buy these to start with. They are light in section, well balanced, and come sharpened ready for use.

The British-made Ashley Iles carving tools are a little less expensive, but are highly recommended. Other makes of carving tool that have received good reviews are Robert Sorby and Crown Tools although I have no personal experience of using them.

All these makes of gouge come sharpened, ready to use, and with good quality, shiny steel blades. Be aware that the sweep numbers of these makes do not always correspond. For example an Ashley Iles no. 3 gouge is equivalent to a Swiss 2 (an Ashley Iles 2 is not a gouge, but a skew chisel). If you choose the Swiss make, ask for gouges with short blades, as these are more manageable. However, if these are unobtainable, you can cut about 1in (25mm) from the handle to reduce the overall length of the longer tool.

Straight-bladed gouges (known as London pattern) will be of most use, since they can be used by hand and with a mallet. Those with bent blades and curved spoon ends should be used by hand only. With these, the cutting edge is not in line with the handle, and if they are used with a mallet, you will not be able to control your cuts accurately; worse, the blade may break.

Avoid buying gouges that are not already prepared for use with the bevels ground to the correct angle, as these will need a lot of preparation with a grindstone and then honing on a sharpening stone before they will cut properly. This is not only frustrating, but is also a difficult job for the newcomer, as in trying to achieve the correct bevel angle, it is very easy to overheat the tip of the tool, thus drawing the temper and damaging the blade.

Chisels

You will probably only need chisels if you want to carve lettering or cut the border around a relief carving. I have yet to find the carver's type, referred to as a no. 1 and included in sets of tools, to be of much use, because it has a bevel on each side of the cutting edge, so you cannot tell precisely at what angle you are cutting when using it for lettering. A normal carpenter's bevelled-edge chisel, available from any good tool shop, is much better. This has a

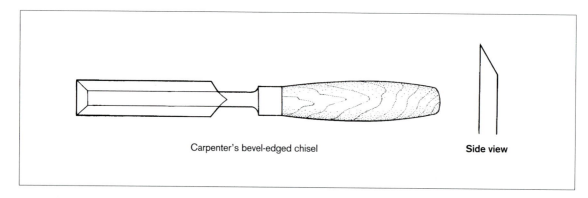

Carpenter's bevel-edged chisel   **Side view**

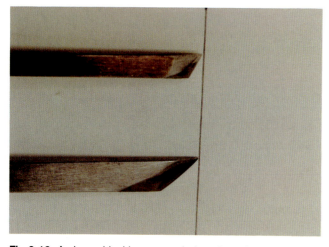

Fig 2.12 A skew chisel has an angled cutting edge with a bevel on both sides. A skew chisel that is too obliquely angled (top) can be re-ground to have a more acute (and more useful) angle (bottom).

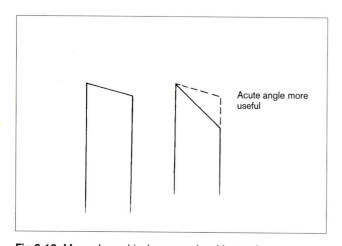

Acute angle more useful

Fig 2.13 Many skew chisels are made with too obtuse an angle to the cutting edge, which makes them impossible to use in confined spaces. An acute angle is more useful.

Fig 2.11 A carver's no. 1 chisel has a straight cutting edge with bevels on both sides, which makes carving lettering difficult. A much better tool is the carpenter's bevelled-edge chisel, which has a bevel on one side of the cutting edge and along both sides of the blade.

flat face with a bevel behind the tip and one along each side of the blade (see Fig 2.11). The firmer chisel, with its rectangular-section blade, is heavier and unwieldy, but just about usable.

In addition, you will need a skew chisel, sometimes called a corner chisel or, if Swiss made, a 1S. This has an angled cutting edge, which ideally should be bevelled on both sides. It is used for tidying up in confined spaces (see Fig 2.12).

The Swiss 1S is the best tool, as it is ready to use. Unfortunately, all the others have a cutting edge set at too shallow an angle. These will require the angle re-grinding to between 30° and 45°, then a bevel re-made on each side of the cutting edge (a difficult job) before you will be able to use the tool (see Fig 2.13).

A bevel on each side of the cutting edge will allow finer cuts to be made; a skew chisel with only one bevel is likely to be too thick and heavy for most purposes. However, such a tool can be useful for cleaning up the transitional areas between the background and the borders of a relief.

V tools

A V tool is used for marking out, cutting channels in end grain, or along the grain, and for texturing; a good one is tremendously useful. As its name implies, it cuts a V-shaped channel by means of its two straight blades, each of which is bevelled on its outer face (see Fig 2.14). V tools are obtainable in angles of 45°, 60° and 90°, but the 60° tool is the most versatile. Note that the chisel number does not indicate the blade angle. For example a London-pattern no. 45 has a blade angle of 90°, so always specify the angle when ordering.

As with gouges, V tools with straight blades are more versatile than those with bent blades, since you can use them with a mallet or by hand. The ¼in (6mm) width is the most useful, this size being the distance between the tips of the blades. Anything larger is likely to be unwieldy, but narrower examples can be useful for texturing hair or fur, and marking out details such as buttons, pockets or creases in clothing.

When choosing a V tool, look at the blades end on. They should be of the same thickness, otherwise one will wear faster than the other, and they should be set at equal angles to an imaginary centreline passing through the point where the blades meet. Turn the tool bevels uppermost and check that along their lengths the blades meet each other sharply, rather than rounded, which will require a very long bevel before it will cut (see Fig 2.15). From side-on, the cutting edges of the blades should be at right angles to its long axis, neither sloping forwards nor back towards the handle, otherwise it will not cut properly (see Figs 2.16 and 2.17).

Fig 2.14 A V tool has a pair of straight-edged blades with a bevel on the underside of each. Various widths are made, while the blades may be set at an angle of 45°, 55°, 60° or 90°.

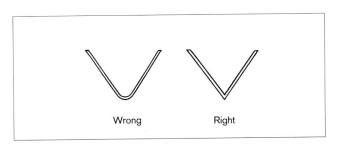

Fig 2.15 The angle between the two blades should be sharp, not rounded off, otherwise the tool will not cut properly.

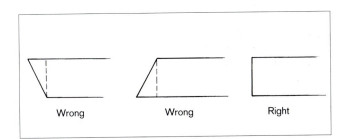

Fig 2.16 When looked at side-on the end of a V tool blade should neither slope forwards nor backwards.

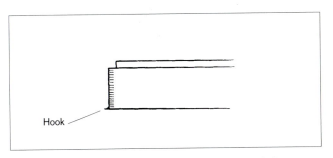

Fig 2.17 With use, a little hook develops in the angle between the blades. Leave this, as it assists the blades in cutting through the wood, particularly when cutting end grain.

15

Fig 2.18 A starter set of carving tools. Top: fine grade ceramic sharpening stone and slipstone. From left to right: mallet; ½in (12mm) no. 9 gouge for removing waste wood quickly; ½in (12mm) no. 2 Swiss (no. 3 British) gouge for smoothing ridges; ¼in (6mm) no. 2 Swiss (no. 3 British) gouge for finer detail; ¼in (6mm) 60° V tool for texturing and marking out relief detail; ¼in (6mm) skew chisel for tidying and finishing; leather strop.

Second-hand tools

If you buy second-hand tools, examine them in the same manner as you would when buying new tools, taking particular note of the condition of the cutting edges. These may be so rusted and pitted that the tools cannot be restored to a usable condition. It may be possible to re-grind the bevel and the edge of a blade, however, then clean it up with wire wool and polish it with metal polishing paste. Check that the handles are sound, and not split, although it is always possible to fit new handles to tools of good quality.

You may find a no. 3 gouge that has been mistakenly sharpened and used as a chisel; the sweep number stamped on the back of the blade will indicate this. In such a case, the tool can be restored using the techniques described in Chapter 3.

You may also find heavy gouges with an inner bevel, usually with a 'shoulder' just before the point where the blade tang enters the handle. These are carpenter's paring or 'in cannel' gouges and are of little use to the carver, as already described. Carver's tools can be distinguished from carpenter's tools, as they do not have the shoulder between the blade and the tang/handle, and they are usually lighter and better balanced.

A starter kit of carving tools

The tools listed here will provide you with a basic kit that will cover most carving needs. It can be expanded as your experience and needs grow. The tools should all be straight-bladed London-pattern types (see Fig 2.18).

Other tools you will need

In addition to gouges and chisels, you will also need a variety of other tools, including sharpening equipment (covered in Chapter 3). Most of these can be bought at a good ironmonger's or tool store. Power tools, such as bandsaws, drills, rotary cutting burrs or routers, are unnecessary for a beginner, making carving a relatively low-cost and quiet activity. At a later date, you will need to acquire an electric grindstone, or gain access to one, unless you know someone who can attend to your tools for you.

Gouges

¼ or ⅜in (6 or 9mm) no. 3 (Swiss no. 2)

½ or ⅝in (13 or 16mm) no. 3 (Swiss no. 2)

½ or ⅝in (13 or 16mm) no. 9

Chisels

¼in (6mm) skew/corner/no. 2 (Swiss 1S)

⅛ or ¼in (3 or 6mm) 60° V tool (Swiss no. 12)

For relief carving, add:

⅛in (3mm) no. 3 gouge (Swiss no. 2)

⅜in (9mm) no. 5 gouge

¾ or 1in (18 or 25mm) carpenter's bevelled-edge chisel

For lettering, add:

A selection of widths of bevelled-edge chisels and a selection of no. 3 (Swiss no. 2) gouges. In fact, the latter will always be useful, and the more of these you have, the better.

Equivalent carving tool numbers

Type of tool	London pattern	Swiss	Type of tool	London pattern	Swiss
Straight chisel	1	1	Gouge	9	9
Skew chisel	2	1S	Gouge	10	–
Gouge	3	2	Gouge	11 half-round	11 U-shape
Gouge	4	3	V tool 60°	39	12
Gouge	5	5	V tool 90°	45	13
Gouge	6	7	V tool 55°	–	14
Gouge	7	8	V tool 45°	41	15
Gouge	8	–			

The tools listed here should meet all your basic needs and can be added to as necessary.

- Mallet; not necessarily a round-headed example.
- Spokeshave with convex sole, or Surform 101A with convex blade.
- Plane, or flat blade for Surform 101A.
- Cabinet scraper; the thinner and more flexible, the better.
- Crosscut saw.
- Coping saw.
- Soft-leaded pencil.
- A device for holding your work securely, such as a bench vice, G-cramps, carver's chops, bench holdfast or Workmate folding bench.
- For relief carving and lettering: an adjustable or try square; for lettering, you will also need a bevel gauge or adjustable protractor.

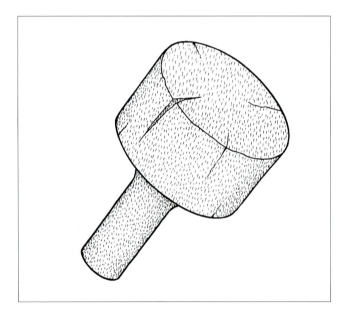

Fig 2.19 If you have access to a lathe, you can turn your own mallet. Make it in one piece from a close-grained hardwood, such as apple. Generally speaking, cracks will not cause any problems.

Mallet

Much of your carving will be done with the aid of a mallet, so a good one is essential. Carver's mallets are normally made of beech, apple or lignum vitae, which is the heaviest, and should be obtainable from the supplier of your carving tools. A mallet should feel comfortable in your hand, but it need not be particularly heavy unless you are carving a very large and hard piece of wood. In fact, the lighter the mallet, the better, as a heavy mallet will require a lot of unnecessary effort to swing. Moreover, since your tools will be sharp, they will not need any great force to drive them through the wood.

Although lignum vitae mallets are more expensive than other types and heavier, size for size, they do wear better. Select one made from the dark heartwood, rather than the yellow sapwood, as it will be harder and more durable.

Avoid any mallet that has a pronounced rounded shape from the top to the bottom of the head, because the tiny surface this presents to the rounded top of the gouge handle may slip off, making the mallet difficult to control. In addition, the blow will not be directed in line with the cutting edge, and you may find great difficulty in actually starting your cuts.

If you know someone who can turn a mallet for you, or have access to a lathe and can do it yourself, it is best to make the handle and head in one piece (see Fig 2.19). That way, there will be no chance of the handle becoming loose. Apple is traditionally used, but any hard close-grained wood will be suitable. You can also use a lathe to turn down

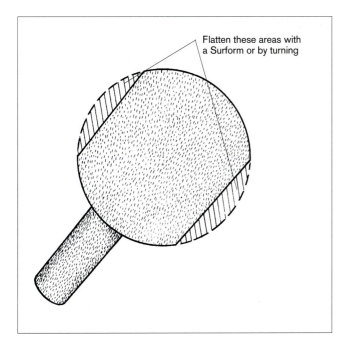

Flatten these areas with a Surform or by turning

Fig 2.20 A very rounded, bulbous mallet may easily slip from the head of a tool handle. Flatten it with a Surform or by re-turning it on a lathe.

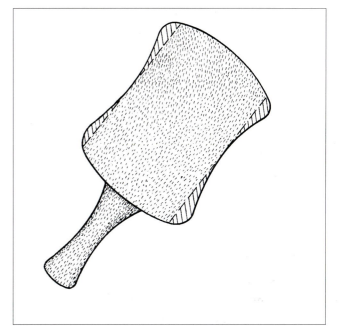

Fig 2.21 A mallet that has become worn can also be reshaped to a smaller diameter with a Surform.

a ready-made mallet that is too bulbous, or you could rasp it with a Surform (see Figs 2.20 and 2.21).

The type of mallet you use is not important, as long as it is comfortable for you. It does not have to be the traditional type; a small carpenter's mallet with a shortened handle will be quite suitable or, like me, you could use a rolled hide type (see Fig 2.22). A mallet becomes an extension of your hand. It should be wielded with an awareness of where the face is striking the tool handle without having to look up from the carving.

Fig 2.22 A heavy mallet can be very tiring to use, especially when working with a large gouge on hard wood. A small, lightweight mallet can often be just as efficient. You could use a carpenter's mallet with the handle shortened, a rolled hide or rubber mallet, or even a mallet made from a log.

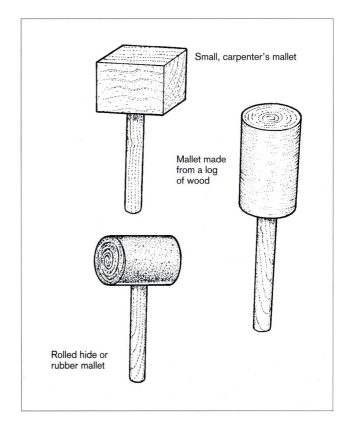

Small, carpenter's mallet

Mallet made from a log of wood

Rolled hide or rubber mallet

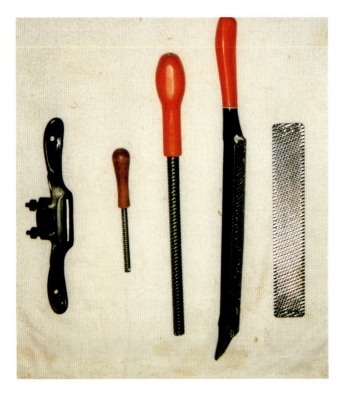

Fig 2.23 From left to right: spokeshave with convex sole; mini surform; ¾in (19mm) standard round surform; surform with a convex blade; flat plane blade for surform.

Spokeshaves, Surforms and planes

If you experience difficulty in using a spokeshave because of its small size, the larger Surform, fitted with a convex blade, will work just as well in many situations (see Fig 2.23). The latter can be used for removing waste wood and rough shaping. It acts rather like a cheese grater, rasping away the wood. It is not a particularly pleasant tool to use, however, as it leaves a rough surface, but it does remove wood quickly, enabling one to get on with the carving. The longer 101A type is easier to handle than the plane-shaped version. It is used with a pushing action, working across and around the shape of the carving. It is now possible to buy miniature versions of these tools for small work.

The spokeshave takes off tiny shavings, leaving a smoother surface, but is considerably slower than the Surform when removing a large amount of waste wood. It can be used in confined spaces where the Surform would be too cumbersome. Buy one with a convex-shaped sole, as this will be of greater use than the flat-soled type, allowing you to work over rounded shapes more easily. Double screw adjusters are better than the single screw type, as they make it easier to adjust the projection of the blade. The spokeshave can be used by either pulling it towards you or pushing it away.

The sole of a spokeshave will have been left rough by the manufacturer, so polish it using the side of a slipstone, followed by Autosol metal polishing paste or a Japanese polishing stone. This will make it much easier to use.

A plane is rarely needed when carving, except for preparing relief wood and levelling the base of a carving in the round. A no. 4 size should suffice. Alternatively, a Surform fitted with the flat blade can be used when levelling the underside of a carving.

The cabinet maker's scraper

These are thin steel plates of various shapes, measuring about 4 x 2in (100 x 50mm), used to smooth a surface, before carving detail, texturing, or finally finishing and abrading.

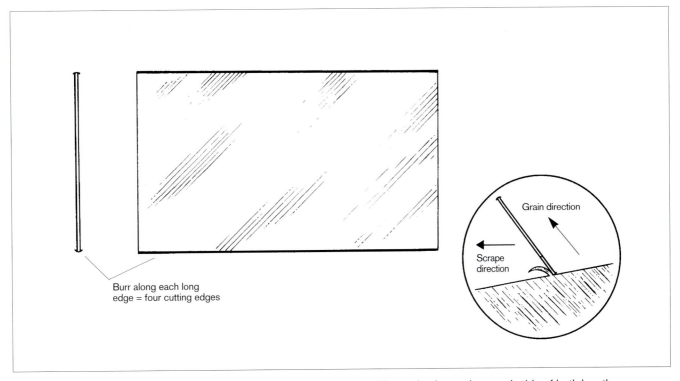

Fig 2.24 The cabinet maker's scraper has cutting edges formed by turning burrs along each side of both lengths.

They are also used to clean up meeting edges.

The cutting edges of this tool run along both faces of the long sides, giving four edges altogether. They are made by turning the metal along each edge to form a burr, which does the cutting (see Fig 2.24). Choose one that is thin and flexible, as a thick scraper will be awkward and tiring to use, while obtaining a good sharp edge will also be difficult. When held by one corner and tapped or flicked, it should give a clear ring.

The scraper is used with a pushing action. To prevent its corners from scoring the surface being cleaned, round them with a file, or run each across a grindstone. When not in use, keep it wrapped in a duster or in a protective plastic holder.

Saws

A crosscut saw, about 20in (50cm) long, will be of most use for cutting away waste wood. Any reputable make will do. A coping saw will also be useful for removing smaller pieces from more complicated carvings.

Pencil

A soft-leaded pencil is essential for marking your work and indicating the direction in which the grain runs, so that you do not cut against it. Do not use a felt-tipped pen, as it penetrates too deeply, nor a ballpoint pen, because this will leave an impression on the wood.

Holding your work securely

It is most important to have some means of holding your work securely, so that it cannot slip or move as you cut. Never hold the carving in one hand while carving with the other; always work so that both hands are behind the cutting edge of the tool. This will prevent you from accidentally gashing your hand, or worse.

A good, firm stable surface is essential to work on, such as a steady table, a solid workbench fitted with a vice, or the heavy-duty version of the Workmate. If the bench shudders or moves as you work, place it up against a wall or put several heavy concrete blocks on its base to steady it.

Since you will be spending hours at your bench, it must be of the correct height and, if necessary, it can be raised by placing the feet on blocks. A comfortable height for carving is somewhere between your wrist and elbow, when standing. A stool will also be useful. Make sure that there is sufficient space for you to move around your work easily without being tempted to cut towards yourself.

A suitable environment

If you can devote a room to your carving, so much the better. For your own comfort in winter, it is best to heat the room. This will also help prevent your tools from rusting, but be careful if using an LPG heater, as this will produce a lot of moisture that can condense on steel blades and cause them to rust. Keep your carvings cool when not working on them, however, as they can split if subjected to a sudden change in temperature.

Make sure your workplace is properly lit, and insulate it for sound if your neighbours are very close. Stand the bench on thick matting or carpet to help absorb sound. If necessary, the noise of your mallet tapping can be muffled by covering the tool's face with leather, held in place with rubber bands. It also helps to wrap, or rest, your carving in a thick towel when working.

Wood chips are clean and do not present a problem as far as dust and dirt are concerned. If you have no special room set aside for carving, lay an old sheet around your bench to collect the chips. Sweep up and dispose of them frequently so that you do not slip on them underfoot, and always keep your working area free of clutter.

Chapter 3

How to Sharpen & Care For Your Tools

Caring for carving tools

If you take care of your carving tools, they will repay you well. To protect their edges, keep your gouges and chisels in a canvas roll, each with its own pocket, or in a felt-lined box with clips to hold them in place.

Do not keep your tools in a metal container, as this can attract condensation and damage their edges if they rattle about inside. Always dry them well after sharpening to prevent rusting, especially if you use a waterstone. If you don't expect to use them for a while, store them in a dry place and spray them with a moisture-repellent spray, such as WD40. Alternatively, include silica crystals or a block of chalk.

Store a plane on its side, not on the sole, which can damage the projecting blade. It is better to hang up saws, rather than lay them flat.

Sharpening carving tools

If your carving is to be enjoyable and safe, your tools must be razor sharp. This is essential, as it is impossible to carve properly with tools that are blunt or that have ragged cutting edges. Moreover, although it may come as a surprise, the sharper your tools, the less likely you are to cut yourself. A sharp tool requires less force to make a cut than a blunt one, so there is less likelihood of it slipping and causing an accident.

Sharpen your tools regularly, ideally before each carving session, and do not regard the time spent doing so as wasted; it will be time well spent, since pushing dull tools through wood is hard work. Some types of wood (such as walnut, teak and yew) dull tools more quickly than others.

There is no mystique to sharpening tools; it is simply a matter of learning the appropriate techniques, which are set out in this chapter. Once you have mastered them, you will find that even old battered and neglected tools can have their cutting edges restored and be given a new lease of life.

Recognizing when your tool is blunt

It is possible to work on and on, not realizing that the tool you are using has become blunt; the first sign is weariness! So if you find your carving becoming tiring, stop and re-sharpen your tools.

As you work, observe the cuts you make. If you notice a series of small ridges or lines that always appear in the same place within each cut (even if you have sharpened the tool recently), this is probably because the burr formed on the cutting edge during sharpening has not been removed completely, or because the cutting edge is nicked. Both will cause the wood fibres to be ripped out, rather than cut cleanly. Hold the tool to the light and you should be able to see the damage.

Fig 3.1 Each time a tool is sharpened, a little of its cutting edge is lost. The result is a short bevel with a slightly rounded profile. Eventually, this must be ground back to produce a bevel of the correct length and profile.

Soft woods will show the marks of a blunt tool very clearly, and often the wood fibres will cling to the cutting edge. Re-sharpen the tool, using the slipstone thoroughly to remove the burr. If the cutting edge has a deep nick in it, the blade will need re-grinding to remove it and the edge re-sharpening on the stone again.

No matter how careful you are, each time a tool is sharpened, the cutting edge bevel angle will be altered imperceptibly. In time, it will become shorter and rounded (see Fig 3.1). This will cause the blade to act like a wedge when it is driven into the wood, making it difficult to use (see Fig 3.2). Re-sharpening the tool will make no difference, and actually aggravates the situation. In this case, the only solution is to re-grind, extending the bevel angle, and then re-sharpen.

If a gouge proves difficult to cut with, even though its bevel is correct and you have honed the tool properly, examine the inside curve of

Fig 3.2 A bevel that is too short will not cut properly because its heel (furthest from the cutting edge) will obstruct the passage of the blade through the wood. A tool with a thick-section blade requires a longer bevel than one with a thin blade. The solution is to re-grind and extend the bevel, using a revolving grindstone.

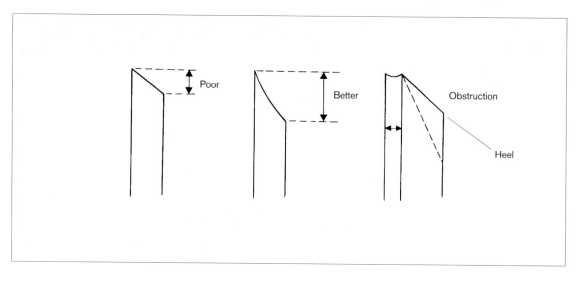

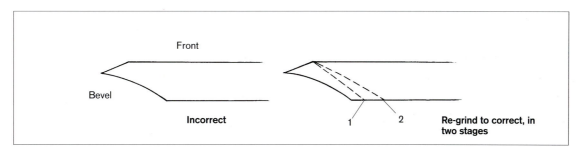

Fig 3.3 If a gouge has been given a bevel along the inside of the cutting edge, it will be very difficult to use, as this second bevel will tend to make the blade dig into the wood, rather than scoop it out. To correct this, the edge will need grinding back beyond the second bevel and a new bevel ground in the correct position underneath.

the cutting edge. The slipstone may have been mishandled and formed a slight bevel or slope towards the cutting edge, which will make the blade dig in, rather than act with a scooping action. The only solution is to grind back the cutting edge to remove the inner bevel, as shown in Fig 3.3, then to re-grind the outer bevel correctly and then re-sharpen it.

Fig 3.4 To sharpen your carving tools, you will need a sharpening stone, slipstones and a leather strop. You will also require the correct lubricant for the stones (either oil or water) and a cloth to wipe the stones clean. If you want absolutely perfect cutting edges, use a ceramic stone or add Japanese polishing stones.

Equipment for sharpening

See Fig 3.4. To sharpen your tools you will need:

- A sharpening stone.
- A slipstone.
- Lubricant (oil or water, depending on the type of sharpening stone and slipstone).
- A cloth for cleaning the stones after use.
- A leather strop.
- A polishing stone and slipstone (optional, but essential for superb edges).

Carving tools are sharpened by honing the bevel on the lubricated sharpening stone, which forms a burr or wire edge across the cutting edge. The latter is removed with the slipstone if you are sharpening a gouge, or the sharpening stone if the tool has a flat blade. Finally, the sharpened edge is wiped on the leather strop to remove any metal particles that may linger.

Sharpening stones

Good sharpening equipment is essential if your tools are to have the razor-sharp cutting edges they require. There are many kinds of sharpening stone, or benchstone as they are often called, and the prices vary. I recommend a fine grade ceramic stone, which is very hard-wearing, but quite expensive. A cheaper alternative is a Japanese waterstone, which gives very good results.

When buying a stone, do not choose one smaller than 6 x 2in (15 x 5cm), as it will be too small for the larger tools. Some stones are man-made, others are natural stones. Some need oil for lubrication, while others depend on water, and the ceramic stones are used dry. You must use the correct lubricant for your stone, otherwise you will spoil it. The finer the stone grade, the better the edge you will obtain.

Some stones are known as combination stones, in that the surfaces are of different grades. Generally speaking, the finer face should be used for carving tools. Most of the artificial stones can be bought in good tool shops and are normally oilstones. The more specialized waterstones and ceramic stones can usually be obtained from a carving tool supplier, along with the shaped slipstones that will fit inside your gouges.

You may come across old sharpening stones in flea markets and second-hand shops, but reject them if chipped, cracked or badly worn. They are likely to be filthy, but can be scrubbed clean with a hard nailbrush, warm water and detergent. If the face is badly worn, the stone may still be usable if prised from its box and turned over. Shallow scrapes and scratches can often be removed by rubbing the damaged surface on 'wet or dry' silicon carbide paper, laid on a sheet of glass or similar completely flat surface. Rub the stone with a circular movement against the abrasive, using water as a lubricant, but be warned: this is a filthy job, and it is a better idea to buy a more up to date type of stone.

The Japanese waterstone requires water as a lubricant and is less messy to use than the conventional oilstone. It is also much cheaper. It should be soaked in water before using, but do not store it in water for long periods, as the faces will become soft, and the water green and smelly. Use a 1,200 grit stone for sharpening carving tools. It is now possible to buy combination Japanese waterstones with 1,000/6,000 faces, the latter being used for polishing. The drawback with Japanese waterstones is that they are fairly soft, and wear hollowed, so need relatively frequent replacement. As I have already mentioned, a fine grade ceramic whetstone avoids this type of problem, being very hard wearing, and giving a finely polished edge to tools, to the extent that you will not need an additional polishing stone.

Slipstones

If possible, a slipstone should always be of the same type and grade as the sharpening stone. However, if you cannot obtain the correct slipstone, it is possible to cut a ¼in (6mm) strip from a Japanese waterstone with a hacksaw or angle grinder fitted with a cutting disc. As these stones are soft enough to shape, round off the edge of the piece to fit the inner curve of your gouges by abrading it along a file or Sandvik sanding plate.

The multiform type of slipstone is the most versatile, as it is tapered along one edge and will fit most sizes of gouge. Normally, it will be about 4in (10cm) long, and smaller examples are quite rare. For smaller gouges, therefore, a Japanese waterstone type can be sawn in two, using a coping saw or hacksaw (the blade will need discarding afterwards) or by scoring a line around the stone (perhaps with a tile cutter) and snapping it cleanly along the scored line with a sharp tap from a mallet. By cutting off a third of the stone's length, the two resulting pieces will be far more useful with short-bladed tools than a full-length stone, which will be too long. It is also possible to buy small Arkansas and India slipstones, which should be soaked in oil before use. As ceramic slipstones are difficult to obtain, a good alternative is the 6,000 or 8,000 grit Japanese slipstones, which can be used wet or dry.

When sharpening a V tool, you will need a very fine-edged slipstone that will reach into the angle between the two blades, and it is possible to buy a knife-edged slipstone for this purpose. If you have a waterstone type of slipstone, you can abrade the tapered edge so that it will fit between the blades by rubbing it along a file or a Sandvik plate, or against the side of your sharpening stone, lubricating it with water.

It is possible to buy a very fine-edged ceramic slipstone which fits a V tool.

Polishing stones

If you want to obtain a really superior polished cutting edge, treat it with a Japanese polishing stone and slipstone after the initial honing. Available in 8,000 and 6,000 grit grades, they are yellow in colour and very soft. When used with a little water, they will give a very superior cutting edge. Although to be recommended, they are fairly expensive as a separate stone. However, you will not need one if you are using a ceramic or a 1,000/6,000 combination Japanese waterstone.

Caring for sharpening stones

Always keep sharpening stones and slipstones clean. Store them in a box, or wrapped in a clean towel or duster. Ideally, mount a sharpening stone in its own box, with a lid, so that it cannot move about when in use. Alternatively, rest it on a damp cloth, or fasten it in a vice. If your Japanese waterstone becomes glazed – usually due to it not being cleaned after use – it can be restored by lubricating and rubbing the surface using the side of your slipstone, or another stone of the same grade.

The strop

A strop is simply a piece of leather, the rough side of which is used for wiping the cutting edge of a newly sharpened tool to remove any metal particles that may remain. Some carvers advocate using a special strop paste as well, but I have not found that it makes much difference to the finished cutting edge if the tool has been polished beforehand.

Sharpening machines

If you have a lot of gouges and chisels to sharpen, you will find it less time consuming to use a powered sharpening machine. This comprises an electric motor fitted with a felt or leather wheel, to which a special abrasive paste is applied (see Fig 3.5). The tool is pressed against the wheel while it is rotating to sharpen and polish the cutting edge. Be careful when using these machines, as it is very easy to overheat the cutting edge and draw the temper, so damaging the tool.

Unfortunately, these machines are quite expensive and, every so often, you will find it necessary to revert to the conventional manual sharpening method to maintain each tool's cutting edge. This is because constant use of the wheel makes the cutting edge so fine that it will break up, becoming 'feathered'. The result will be tiny scratches and flawed cuts in your workpiece, particularly visible in soft woods such as lime. Honing in the conventional way removes this damaged edge.

Fig 3.5 A powered sharpener will be useful if you have a lot of tools to sharpen, but from time to time you will have to revert to manual sharpening. The reason for this is that the sharpener will produce a very fine cutting edge that will eventually break up.

Types of sharpening stone, in order of coarseness

■ Silicon carbide: green, man-made, oil lubricated.

■ Carborundum: grey/black, oil lubricated.

■ India: orange/brown, man-made, oil lubricated (soak in oil before use). Select the fine grade for carving tools; anything else is too coarse.

■ Slate: grey, green, black or purple, oil or water lubricated (oil seems to work better). Very soft and wear quickly if not treated carefully.

■ Japanese waterstone: orange, water lubricated (soak well in water before use). Available from specialist tool suppliers in 800, 1,000 and 1,200 grit grades.

■ Arkansas: soft grey, hard white and hard black, oil lubricated. Naturally occurring stones that shatter if dropped and are expensive.

■ Japanese polishing stone: 6,000 or 8,000 grit (grey or yellow respectively), very soft, water lubricated. Rather expensive on their own, but the 6,000 grit is now available as one face of a combination 1,000/6,000 stone.

■ Diamond: very hard, with the appearance of perforated mesh. Rather expensive, used dry.

■ Ceramic: white, very hard, man-made synthetic sapphires, available in medium, fine and ultrafine grades. Use fine for carving tools. Used dry, no lubrication needed, very hard-wearing, giving a high polish to the cutting edge.

Sharpening techniques

Saws

A sharp saw will create tiny curls of wood, not dust, cutting quickly and cleanly with a crisp sound. Its teeth should be shiny and set correctly, otherwise you will find difficulty in sawing along a line. Sharpening a saw involves using a file across the teeth, and there are various saw setting and sharpening devices on the market that simplify the process. However, it can be a noisy, anti-social task, so you may prefer to buy an inexpensive saw and simply replace it when it becomes blunt. Some cheap saws actually come with specially hardened teeth that have a long life and cannot be sharpened anyway.

An alternative to sharpening a saw yourself is to send it to a saw doctor, who will set and sharpen the teeth for you. A good ironmonger's or tool shop will offer this service.

Straight-bladed gouges

When honing a gouge, the sharpening stone should be parallel to the edge of your bench, and you should make sure that it cannot slip. A Japanese waterstone should be soaked well in water first; when it has stopped 'fizzing', it will be ready for use. Remove it from the water and rub your slipstone over the surface to produce a paste, which will improve its sharpening action, as well as removing any glaze.

Apply plenty of lubricant to the stone, stand directly in front of it and place the right-hand edge of the gouge bevel on the top left-hand corner of the stone. Hold the

Fig 3.6 When sharpening a gouge, hold the handle of the tool in your right hand and steady the blade with the index and middle fingers of your left hand. The blade should be at an angle of approximately 27°, so that the cutting edge is in contact with the stone.

gouge handle in your right hand and tilt the tool until it is at 27° to the horizontal, when, where the edge is in contact with the surface of the stone, you will see a line of moisture along the edge of the tool. Steady the blade with the index and middle fingers of your other hand, as shown in Fig 3.6.

Keeping your elbows into your sides, rotate the gouge by rolling your wrists and simultaneously draw it diagonally across the stone to the lower right-hand corner. During this movement, almost the entire width of the cutting edge should come into contact with the stone, and you should finish with the left-hand edge of the bevel on the stone.

Now, slide the gouge up to the top right-hand corner of the stone, keeping the left-hand edge of the bevel in contact with its surface and rolling your wrists slightly to ensure that the entire width of the bevel has been honed. It is essential to maintain the 27° angle while doing this and to take care not to let the corners of the blade dig into the stone, otherwise you will score the surface. You must not let the handle wander sideways, either, as you turn your wrists.

Now repeat the action, but work diagonally from the top right-hand corner to the lower left-hand corner, then up to the top left-hand corner. Rotate the tool as you move it so that the right-hand edge of the gouge bevel ends up at your original starting point. This action should have described a complete figure of eight, and the cutting edge should have been abraded across its full width twice (see Fig 3.7).

When honing, use light even pressure on the stone and take your time. Uneven pressure on one side or the other will give a lop-sided cutting edge, although this can be made good when you next sharpen the tool by applying more pressure on the less worn side. Make the figure of eight as large as possible to spread the wear on the stone, and use plenty of lubricant, otherwise metal may be rubbed into the surface and the stone spoiled. The amount you turn your wrists will depend on the sweep of the gouge: a deeper sweep requires more rotation than a shallow one. However, if you rotate the tool too much, the corners will dig in and be rounded off, while if you do not turn it enough, a dip will develop in the centre of the cutting edge.

Continue with the figure of eight action until a burr has formed along the inner face of the cutting edge. You can check for this

Fig 3.7 Hone a gouge by moving it with a figure-of-eight action across the face of the sharpening stone, at the same time rolling the tool so that the whole width of the edge comes into contact with the stone twice by the time it returns to the starting point. Begin with the right-hand corner of the edge in contact with the upper left-hand corner of the stone.

by running your fingernail outwards and across the edge. If you feel it catch, the burr has been formed and you have finished honing. On a ceramic or waterstone, this process will not take very long – about six 'figure of eights' should be sufficient, provided you are holding the tool at the correct angle to the stone.

If a burr will not form, you are probably holding the tool at too shallow an angle in relation to the surface of the stone, and the edge is not in contact with it. Tip it up a little to an angle greater than 27° and repeat the honing action (see Fig 3.8). This will occur as the bevel of the gouge wears through use and regular sharpening. It must be compensated for by holding the tool more steeply when honing it, until the tool is re-ground correctly.

After honing, wipe the stone so that it is completely clean, otherwise the slurry will sink in and damage the surface.

All traces of the burr must be removed if the tool is to cut properly. This is done by rubbing flat along the inside of the blade with the slipstone (see Fig 3.9).

Rest the gouge blade on the bench so that the ferrule is pressed firmly against the edge. Hold the handle in one hand and with the other place the lubricated slipstone inside the curve of the blade, so that it overhangs the cutting edge by about ½in (1.25cm). Rub the slipstone back and forth, about ½in (1.25cm) in each direction, at the same time moving it across the width of the blade. Keep a steady pressure on the blade throughout and take care not to tip the stone over the cutting edge, which will result in an undesirable bevel inside the curve.

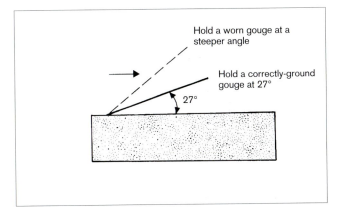

Fig 3.8 With a correctly ground gouge, the blade should be held at approximately 27° when honing. However, if the blade is worn, you may need to increase the angle to get a burr to form.

Fig 3.9 When a burr has formed across the tip of the blade, it will need no further honing. Remove the burr with a slipstone, pressing it firmly against the inside of the gouge blade. Use only the last ½in (1.25cm) of the stone, rubbing it back and forth across the width of the cutting edge. Then strop the blade to remove metal particles.

Continue until the burr has been removed completely, testing with your fingernail. When you think it has gone, continue rubbing for a little longer to be absolutely sure, otherwise the tool may be left with a dull spot.

This method of using a slipstone ensures that your fingers are always safely behind the cutting edge. Do not be tempted to hold the tool in one hand and rub from the cutting edge in towards the handle; always rest the gouge so that it is steady on the bench.

Another check you can make to determine whether the burr has been removed is to hold the tool edge to the light and look along it. The light will be reflected from any remnants of the burr or any dull spot. This is also a good check for blunt or damaged tools.

As with the sharpening stone, wipe the slipstone clean after use.

Wipe both sides of the tool's cutting edge several times along the rough side of the leather, which will remove any metal particles that may still be adhering to it. Then dry the tool carefully, especially if you have been using a waterstone; rust will form surprisingly quickly if you leave any moisture on the blade.

A shiny polished cutting edge will always cut more efficiently because it will generate less friction as it is driven through the wood, so it makes sense to polish the cutting edge if you can. If you have a Japanese polishing stone, either the 8,000 or 6,000 grit type, and the corresponding slipstone, repeat the sharpening and slipstone procedures. This will put a fine polish on the bevel and the tool will cut beautifully. With a ceramic stone, no further polishing after the initial sharpening is necessary.

A good, but less expensive, alternative to polishing stones is to glue a piece of leather to a flat surface, such as a piece of thick plywood, measuring about 8 x 2in (20 x 5cm). Apply some Autosol metal polishing paste, then hone your tool in the paste. You can make a 'slipstone' to fit inside your

gouges by covering a suitably shaped piece of wood with leather in the same way. Apply the paste to this, and polish the curved inner surfaces of your gouges. Autosol is available from car accessory shops.

Bent-bladed gouges

In time, you may acquire gouges with bent blades, their cutting edges being offset either in front of the handle or behind. In both cases, you should sharpen them using the figure of eight technique, but you must hold the tool to compensate for the position of the handle.

With front-bent blades, the handle must be tipped forwards to ensure a 27° angle on the bevel, as shown in Fig 3.10. Watch for

Fig 3.10 When honing a front-bent gouge, the handle will have to be raised to ensure that the edge is in contact with the stone.

the formation of a burr as before, but if none forms, tilt the handle even further forwards. To remove the burr, prop the gouge against a wedge of scrap wood so that the cutting edge is accessible with the slipstone. Then carefully rub into the curve from the cutting edge towards the handle, taking care not to rub across the edge (see Fig 3.11).

With back-bent blades, place the stone so that it lies along the edge of the bench, allowing the handle of the tool to be manipulated from below the level of the stone. Hone the blade along the very edge of the stone, as shown in Fig 3.12, adjusting the handle position as necessary to obtain a burr. Remove this with the slipstone, resting the cutting edge firmly on the bench (see Fig 3.13). Finish off both types of tool with the strop.

Remember that British and Swiss tools are referred to as front or back bent, but their corresponding German counterparts are known back or front bent.

Skew chisels

Place the sharpening stone end on to the edge of the bench and lubricate it well. Stand directly in line with the stone. If the stone is worn, use its side instead.

If the tool has a bevel on both sides, hold it so that the angled cutting edge is parallel to the end of the stone. Hold the bevel flat against the stone, raising the handle of the tool until the blade is at an angle of 13° to the surface of the stone. This can be difficult to estimate, so it is best to think of it as being not quite flat. At the correct angle, a bead of moisture will be visible

Fig 3.11 Prop the gouge on a piece of wood and rub the slipstone back and forth, from the cutting edge towards the handle. Take care not to tilt the slipstone over the cutting edge, otherwise you will alter the cutting angle.

Fig 3.12 When honing a back-bent gouge, place the stone on the very edge of the bench so that the tool's handle can be held below it. The amount by which you drop the handle will depend on the bend of the blade. Hone the gouge with a long, narrow figure of eight or rocking action along the edge of the stone.

Fig 3.13 Rest the blade against the edge of the bench and rub off the burr with a slipstone.

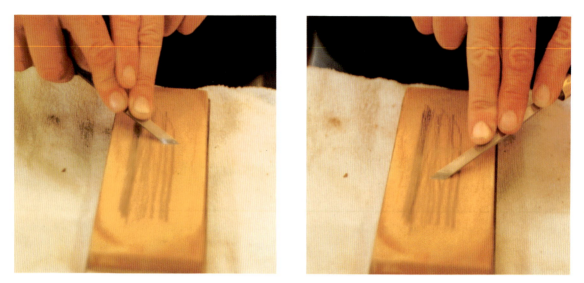

Fig 3.14 When honing a two-bevel skew chisel, hold the tool so that the cutting edge is parallel to the end of the sharpening stone and at an angle of 13°. Rub the blade up and down the whole length and width of the stone. Then turn it over and repeat the same number of strokes for the other bevel. To remove the burr, turn the blade again and draw it towards you a couple more times. Finally, strop the blade, but be careful as it will be very sharp.

along the cutting edge as the tool is honed.

Using light pressure with your fingers, and keeping the cutting edge parallel to the end of the stone, rub the bevel up and down, using the whole width of the stone and taking care not to push the point of the tool into the surface (some carvers prefer to draw the tool towards themselves to do this). Complete about a dozen strokes, then turn the tool over and repeat the process for the other bevel, using the same number of strokes (see Fig 3.14). The first action will put a burr along the cutting edge; the second will remove it and form another burr on the other side of the blade. Turn the blade again and draw the bevel along the stone towards you a couple of times to remove the burr. Finally, wipe both sides of the blade on the strop.

If the tool has a bevel on one side only, proceed as before, but hold the tool at an angle of 27°. When a burr has formed, turn the tool over and place the flat side of the blade against the stone, with about two thirds of its length pressed firmly on the surface. Rub the blade up and down to break off the burr, taking care not to lift the blade from the surface. Then strop as before.

Spokeshaves, planes and bevel chisels

The blades of these tools are all sharpened in the same way. When newly purchased, their bevels may need re-grinding, as they are rarely ready for use. The bevels should be hollow ground to about ⅛in (3mm) in length at an angle of 27°, as described on page 31.

If you are sharpening a spokeshave or plane blade, remove it from the body of the tool by releasing the retaining plate. Then, with the lubricated sharpening stone end-on, hold the blade bevel down at an angle of 27° and rub it up and down until a burr forms. As with a gouge, tilt the tool slightly more if necessary until a bead of moisture is visible along the cutting edge.

Turn the tool over so that the bevel is uppermost, and press the blade flat against the surface of the stone. Rub it back and forth firmly to remove the burr. The sound of the blade being worked across the stone should change slightly when the burr has gone; confirm this by stroking outwards with your fingernail.

Strop the blade as usual. With a spokeshave or plane, replace the blade in its holder, bevel downwards and located properly on its screw ledges. Tighten the retaining plate and adjust the screws until the cutting edge projects slightly beyond the sole of the tool.

V tools

For sharpening purposes, a V tool should be treated as if it is two straight chisels joined together. Hold the tool at 27° to the surface of the lubricated stone, with the cutting edge of one blade against the stone and parallel with the end. Rub the bevel up and down until a burr is formed. Repeat this procedure for the other blade, using the same number of strokes to ensure that both are evenly honed and one will not wear faster than the other.

To remove the burr, use a knife-edged slipstone or a reshaped standard slipstone that will reach right into the angle between the blades. Rest the tool on the bench, with its ferrule against the edge. Press the flat side of the slipstone against the inner surface of one of the blades and, using the last ½in (1.25cm) of it, rub back and forth, keeping the pressure against the blade (see Fig 3.15). Repeat for the other blade and strop as normal.

If the V tool has a bent blade, sharpen it in the same manner, but tilt it forwards to compensate for the bend in the blade.

If the hook that eventually develops between the two blades becomes troublesome and impedes the cutting action of the tool, you can remove it by honing the blade as if it is a tiny gouge, using a figure of eight action. Then remove the burr with a sharply-pointed slipstone, after which both blades should be sharpened as described above.

If you find that one blade wears more quickly than the other, this may be because it is thinner due to a manufacturing error. However, this may also occur if you are putting more pressure on that blade when honing it.

Fig 3.15 To remove the burrs from a V tool, use a knife-edged slipstone, pressing it firmly against the inside of each blade and rubbing it back and forth.

Sharpening by machine

When using a powered sharpener, stand directly in front of the wheel and switch the machine on. Warm up the wheel by pressing a small piece of emery paper against it; wrapping the paper around a length of dowel will prevent you from burning your fingers. Then apply a generous amount of abrasive paste to the wheel while it is revolving. Do this from above spindle level so that it is not flicked into your face.

Press the gouge firmly against the wheel, holding it at an angle of 27°, and quickly turn the cutting edge from the centre of its curve towards the outer edge of the wheel in one direction, then back again in the other so that the full width of the cutting edge is abraded. Keep a continuous firm pressure on the wheel, but do not overheat the edge by pressing too hard, or you will damage the tool. You should see a moist black line appear along the cutting edge, which is the abrasive paste being activated by friction. This is sufficient to sharpen and polish the cutting edge; there is no need to use a slipstone, but strop the blade for the best results.

This method is particularly useful for sharpening narrow-angled V tools and tiny U-shaped gouges, as finding suitable narrow slipstones can be difficult. Rest the blade of the V tool flat against the rotating wheel, gently raise the tool handle until you see the line of moisture across the edge, and repeat for the other blade.

After sharpening your tools, clean the wheel with emery paper wrapped around a dowel while it is rotating. True-up the sides in the same manner.

Sharpening a scraper

A sharp scraper will produce tiny curved shavings as it cuts and will be a joy to use. In many cases, it will need sharpening before it can be used, while a large scraper may need cutting in half with a hacksaw to make it more manageable.

First the long edges of the scraper must be made square to the flat faces. To do this, fasten the scraper lengthways in a vice with one long edge protruding. Run a double-cut file along the edge until it is flat and shiny, as shown in Fig 3.16. Turn the scraper over and repeat for the other edge. Alternatively, run each edge across the wheel of a grindstone.

Next polish the edges by rubbing them across a lubricated sharpening stone, as shown

Fig 3.16 Before sharpening, the edges of a new scraper should be dressed so that they are square to the faces. Clamp the file in a vice and draw each long edge of the scraper along it until it is flat and shiny.

in Fig 3.17. If you use the entire width of the stone, you will not rub a groove in it. Alternatively, use the side of the stone. Continue rubbing until a slurry has formed and the edge is polished. Then turn the scraper over and repeat the process for the other edge.

With a coarse sharpening stone, you may find that a burr has formed along each side of the cutting edge. These burrs can be removed by flattening the faces in the same manner as sharpening a plane or spokeshave blade. Place one end of the scraper flat on the stone, hold the other end and firmly rub the face up and down until a change of note is heard (see Fig 3.18).

A scraper cuts by means of a little hook or burr, which is formed by slightly bending over the metal along the very edge of each long side, using a special burnishing tool available from good tool shops. You can use the polished back of a gouge instead. To do this, fasten the scraper in a vice with one

long edge protruding and exactly parallel with the top of the bench. About a third of the scraper should protrude above the vice jaws. Make sure the vice is very tight, as you will be putting a lot of pressure on the tool.

Select a gouge with a smooth shiny back to it and rest this across the edge of the scraper so that the blade is horizontal, but at right angles to the faces of the scraper, and pointing towards the bench. Hold the gouge handle in your right hand, steadying the blade with the index, middle and third fingers of your left. Press the back of the gouge blade firmly against the edge of the scraper. Now lift the handle by 5–10°.

Keeping your fingers well away from the end of the gouge blade, push the tool firmly along the edge of the scraper and away from you at the same time. Keep a steady angle and pressure until you reach the end of the scraper. If you find this difficult, or you slip off the end, try rubbing the gouge back and

Fig 3.17 Hold the scraper perfectly upright on the lubricated sharpening stone. Then rub it up and down, moving across the stone and back, to polish the edges.

Fig 3.18 Remove the burrs from the scraper edges by laying it flat on the stone and rubbing it up and down.

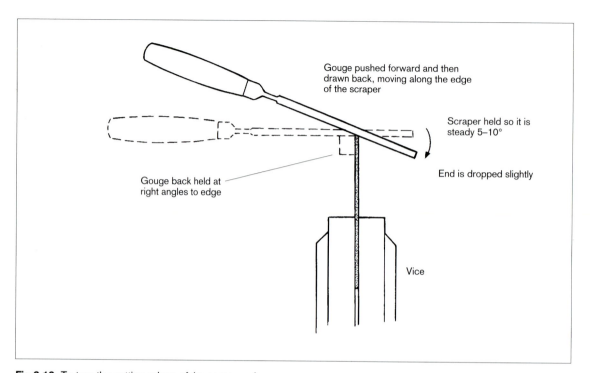

Gouge pushed forward and then
drawn back, moving along the edge
of the scraper

Scraper held so it is
steady 5–10°

Gouge back held at
right angles to edge

End is dropped slightly

Vice

Fig 3.19 To turn the cutting edges of the scraper, clamp it in a vice and hold the back of a gouge at right angles to the top edge. Raise the handle of the gouge slightly, then push the gouge back and forth while moving along the edge of the scraper. This will turn a small hook shape on the corner of the edge. Turn the scraper around and repeat the process for the other corner. Then treat the other long edge in the same manner.

forth as you move it along the edge, to give you more control (see Fig 3.19). Maintain the angle and pressure until you reach the end of the scraper. You should be able to feel a tiny burr along the edge of the scraper with your fingernail.

Turn the scraper around, but with the same edge uppermost, and repeat the procedure to produce a second burr. Then remove the scraper and form two more burrs on the other long edge. In the correct light, you can see these burrs being formed as you press with the gouge.

As the scraper is used, it will become blunt (some woods, such as yew, walnut and teak, will cause this more rapidly than others), producing dust rather than shavings. To re-sharpen it, you will have to polish the edges again and form new burrs. If the edges become badly worn or out of true, they will need filing or grinding back to shape.

Re-grinding with a grindstone

Various types of grindstone are available, but the best will have a wheel that revolves through a water trough. This will prevent you from drawing the temper of the blade by overheating it. However, you can manage without a water trough if you dip the blade into cool water after each stroke across the wheel.

Grinding is a messy, unpleasant job, so

wear protective clothing, including plastic gloves if you do not want metal to become ingrained in your skin. Proper goggles, not spectacles, are essential, even though the machine will have eye shields. Never use the sides of the wheel to grind tools, and keep all inflammable items well away from the machine, especially if the wheel is not the type that revolves in water, as impressive quantities of sparks can be produced. If the surface of the wheel becomes glazed or out of true, it must be re-dressed, either with a diamond dresser pencil or a dressing wheel, both of which can be bought from good tool shops.

When grinding, use light pressure and do not force the tool against the wheel. Make sure the wheel is correctly balanced within its shield, and always use the tool rest. A magnet placed in the water bath will collect metal particles so that the water remains clean, while a drop of washing-up liquid in the water helps prevent metal particles from settling on the surface of the wheel and glazing it.

To re-grind the bevel on a gouge, hold the tool in your right hand and place the index finger of your left hand on the tool rest, about ½in (1.25cm) away from the wheel. Rest the gouge on your finger, holding the handle low. Steady the blade by holding it down on your finger with light pressure from your left thumb.

As a general rule, the length of the bevel should be approximately half the width of the blade, and you should begin grinding at this distance back from the cutting edge. With a very wide tool, however, this rule of thumb will need modifying, or you will have to remove an enormous amount of metal. Roll the tool across its width, at the same time moving it across the width of the wheel. This is done by turning the right hand and wrist (see Fig 3.20). The left hand should be held firmly against the tool rest to control the angle at which the tool is moved. If necessary, after each pass across the wheel, cool the blade by dipping it in water.

If too much pressure is applied to the tool, or the cutting edge remains in contact

Fig 3.20 Control the angle of the blade with your left hand and rotate the tool against the grinding wheel by rolling your right wrist and hand. When re-grinding a chisel, no rotation of the blade is necessary; simply pass it from side to side.

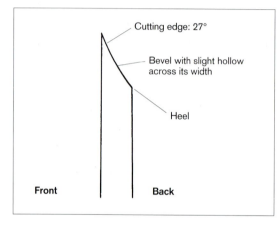

Fig 3.21 (above) Re-grinding commences at the heel (left) and is continued forwards towards the edge (right), whilst rotating the tool across the width of the stone.

Fig 3.22 (left) A correctly ground bevel will have a slight hollow behind the cutting edge and across its full width. This eases passage of the blade through the wood.

with the wheel for too long, it will become blued, which is a clear indication that it has been overheated. This will soften the cutting edge and ruin the tool. To be of any use, the blade will have to be re-tempered, which is beyond the scope of this book. However, an engineering or blacksmith's shop should be able to do this for you. (It is also possible to ruin tools in this way when sharpening by machine, if you are not careful).

Continue to make passes across the wheel, gradually raising the handle as you do so and working towards the cutting edge (see Fig 3.21). Slowly remove the metal, but stop just before you reach the very tip of the cutting edge. At this point, grind away a little more metal to hollow the bevel

slightly, as shown in Fig 3.22. This shape will ensure an easy passage of the tool through the wood, reducing the friction generated and the force needed to work it. You should aim to achieve a shallow angle of about 27°, which is the most efficient.

After grinding, the blade should be sharpened and polished in the usual way, using sharpening stone, slipstone and strop.

If the gouge fails to cut properly and you are sure that you did not draw the temper by overheating the steel, it is likely that insufficient metal has been removed from behind the cutting edge and the bevel needs more hollowing. Alternatively, the bevel may not be long enough and will need taking further back along the blade, which is likely if the tool has been manufactured too thick in section.

A straight chisel is ground in the same

manner, but is not rolled as it passes over the wheel. Draw it across in a straight line, keeping the bevel surface flat against the wheel. As before, use the tool rest to ensure that the blade is held steadily and accurately against the wheel. Some grindstones can be fitted with jigs that ensure the correct blade angle for most tools.

Dealing with nicks and damaged or misshapen edges

If there is a deep nick in the cutting edge of a tool, or a corner has broken off, or the edge becomes badly misshapen through careless sharpening, the tip of the blade will need straightening before a bevel can be re-ground on it. The same applies to a gouge with a bevel on the inside of its blade, or a V tool that has blade tips leaning forwards or backwards. Most second-hand tools will need similar treatment, as will carving tools that are not sold 'ready sharpened'.

Hold the tool as described, but place the index finger of your left hand under the tool rest so that the blade is laid flat on the rest. Position your right hand so that the blade is horizontal. Run the tip of the blade across the wheel until you have squared it off, cooling it after each stroke. Then form a bevel in the normal manner.

Re-grinding a skew chisel

Most skew chisels, other than Swiss examples, will need their cutting edges re-grinding to a more acute angle to be of any

use. A cutting edge angle of 30–45° is preferable so that the tool will reach into confined spaces. It will also need shallower bevels to cut properly.

Draw a guide line across the tip of the blade at the desired angle, using a pencil. Then hold the blade flat against the rest and remove metal down to the line. Be very careful not to blue the end of the blade, as the metal will be very thin at this point.

The bevels can then be re-ground in the normal manner, but the angle of each should be as close to 13° as possible. The bevels should also be hollowed slightly so that the tool cuts easily. Finally, sharpen the chisel in the normal manner (see Fig 3.23). Again, if you find difficulty in cutting with the tool, hollow the bevels slightly more and re-sharpen. If the problem persists, extend the bevel lengths and re-sharpen.

Re-grinding a V tool

When re-grinding a V tool, treat each blade as if it is a straight chisel. At the point where the bevels meet on the underside of

Fig 3.23 Re-grinding a new bevel on the altered cutting edge of a skew chisel.

the tool, you may have to reduce the metal, depending on its overall thickness. Do not forget that the ends of the blade must lean neither forwards nor backwards.

As usual, the angle of each bevel should be about 27° and, as far as possible, they should be of the same length, otherwise the tool will be difficult to control and one blade may wear faster than the other (see Fig 3.24). If the tool refuses to cut properly, it is most likely that the metal where the two blades meet is too thick. Carefully reduce this by grinding, slightly rolling the tool from side to side to elongate the bevel along the angle. Then re-sharpen the tool.

Restoring an incorrectly sharpened gouge

It is very easy to mistake a gouge with a shallow sweep, such as a no. 3 or Swiss 2, for a chisel and, thus, sharpen it incorrectly, damaging the cutting edge. You may find that this has occurred when buying second-hand tools. If there is no number stamped on the blade to confirm that the tool is a gouge, examine the blade end on, looking for the shallow curve, or press the tip into a piece of paper to see if it leaves a curved impression.

If the tool is a gouge, you will have to restore the cutting edge. First, lay the blade on the bench with its ferrule against the edge. Then, using a lubricated slipstone, begin to rub a gentle hollow across the width of the cutting edge. Rub back and forth, keeping the pressure of the slipstone firmly on the inside of the blade so that no more than ½in (1.25cm) extends beyond the

cutting edge. This will prevent the slipstone from tilting over the cutting edge and altering the cutting angle.

Work methodically across the width of the blade and back again. Pay particular attention to the two outer corners because these will have been flattened when the tool was sharpened as a chisel. Try to maintain an even curve across the width of the blade, and do not spend longer on one area than another. Do not use a powered abrasive stone to create this curve, as it may produce an unwanted inner bevel.

Once the curve has been restored, the bevel will need re-grinding to a corresponding curve. Then the tool can be sharpened in the normal manner.

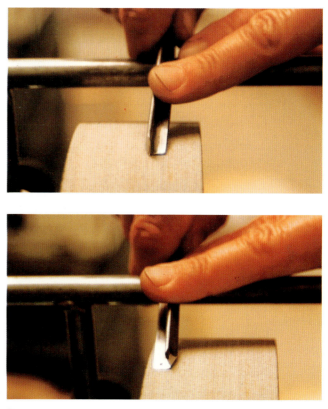

Fig 3.24 Re-grinding a new bevel on each blade of a V tool.

Chapter 4

How to Use Your Tools Correctly

Many aspiring carvers initially find some difficulty in manipulating woodcarving tools, but once they have learned how to use these unfamiliar implements, their confidence grows and their carvings develop. This chapter will show you how to use the various carving tools efficiently and competently, allowing you to translate many ideas into wood and opening up a whole new world where the only limit will be your imagination.

Saws

Before you begin any carving, you will need a suitable piece of wood, and to cut it to length you will need a crosscut saw. When marking the piece out, try to arrange it so that you can saw directly downwards along the marked line, rather than at an angle. It will be difficult to control the saw if the blade is not held vertically, as the weight of the blade will not assist the cutting action.

Having marked out the wood, fasten it firmly in the vice or to the top of your bench with a G-cramp. Alternatively, rest it on a bench hook, but clamp the end of the hook in the vice to prevent it from wandering while you are sawing.

You must hold the saw correctly, with

Fig 4.1 When using a saw, secure your wood in a vice or to the bench with G-cramps. Stand with your shoulder, elbow and forearm directly in line with the saw, and your index finger pointing along the handle to prevent the saw from wobbling. Prop the blade against the thumb of your free hand when starting the cut, then move your hand back out of the way to steady the workpiece.

your index finger pointing forwards. This will allow you to control the sideways movement of the blade. Stand so that your sawing arm is directly in line with the saw.

To start the cut, rest your other hand on the wood with your thumb lying along the line to be cut. Prop the saw against your thumb and draw the blade back towards you a few times to form a groove, or kerf, which will prevent the blade from wandering (see Fig 4.1). Then begin the back-and-forth sawing action,

43

having moved your hand away from the line of cut, but keeping it on the wood to steady it.

Make the first few strokes quite short so that you follow the guide line accurately. Then gradually increase the length of your strokes until the full length of the blade is being used. This will not only speed the cut, but also ensure an even wear pattern on the teeth. While sawing, keep your hand, forearm, elbow and shoulder in line, and saw with a steady unhurried rhythm. Keep your eye on the guide line, and if the saw should wander off, gently twist it to guide it back. When nearing the end of the cut, slow down and hold the waste wood so that it cannot fall to the floor or break off, which may damage the piece you want.

If your saw is sharp and set correctly, it should produce a clean crisp sound and tiny curls of wood as you saw. If it veers to one side and is difficult to control, this may be because the teeth are not set correctly. If the blade chatters, vibrates or squeals as you pull it back, you are not holding it directly in line with the cut you are trying to make, so move until your arm, shoulder, etc. are in line again. If the blade jams, you are pushing too hard and forcing the teeth into the wood. Relax, and let the weight of the saw do the cutting.

When sawing a wide log, you may be tempted to cut through half of it, then turn it around and make a second finishing cut. If you do this, however, you may find that the two cuts do not meet. It is much better to begin the cut as described, then gradually turn the log to continue the kerf until you have a continuous groove all the way round. Keep turning the log as you saw down towards the centre.

Never blow the sawdust away from the wood, since with some woods, such as yew, it may be toxic or an irritant. Instead, brush it aside and sweep it up as soon as you have finished sawing to prevent it from leaving a slippery surface underfoot.

Mallet and gouge techniques

In all carving, use the mallet as much as possible. Not only will this speed up your work, but it will also provide better control of your tools. However, never use a mallet with tools that have bent blades, as it will be difficult to guide them and you may even break the blades. Also, never use your hand instead of a mallet to drive carving tools: at best, this will hurt; at worst, you may even injure yourself.

When using a mallet, work in a steady unhurried manner, tapping the end of the gouge handle smartly, but not with heavy-handed blows. Provided the mallet is used correctly and the gouge blade set in the centre of the handle, the latter will not split; if it does break, this will probably be because you are striking it too harshly.

Hold the gouge firmly in your left hand, well down the tool, so that the end of the handle is exposed and there is no danger of your hand being struck accidentally. The lower you hold the blade, the more control you will have, which is why a gouge with a short blade is preferable to one with a long blade. To help balance the tool, rest your thumb lengthways along the underside of the handle, as shown in Fig 4.2. Keep your gouge hand relaxed when carving, rather than gripping the handle tightly, which will be very tiring, and rest your forearm and wrist on the work where possible.

Some gouges are supplied with handles that are too heavy and unbalanced for the size of blade. These can be reduced to a more manageable diameter by paring down with another gouge (or spokeshave or Surform), or mounting the ferrule in a collar and turning it down on a lathe.

Place the cutting edge of the gouge at the point where you want to begin cutting. Work in the direction of the grain, or very slightly across it. Hold the tool at an angle so that only the centre of the cutting edge will cut into the wood fibres and the corners will be clear, otherwise they will become embedded in the wood, which will split (see Fig 4.3). At the same time, the blade must not be at too shallow an angle, as it will simply slide over the surface and not cut at all.

Begin a series of four or five steady taps with the mallet on the gouge handle. The first tap should be quite sharp so that the cutting edge bites into the wood, then drop your gouge hand slightly so that the gouge lies at a shallower angle. Continue driving it rhythmically and steadily. Unless you are rounding over, in which case you should lift your gouge hand, finish the cut by scooping with your gouge hand to lift out the chip cleanly. Continue tapping as you do this to prevent the chips from

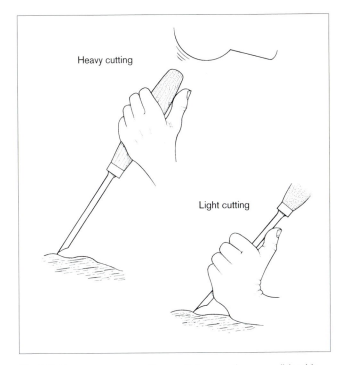

Fig 4.2 Use your gouges with a mallet as much as possible; this will be much quicker than paring by hand. When removing large amounts of wood, hold the gouge handle near the top and strike the end smartly with the mallet. For lighter cutting, when you need more precise control, hold the blade close to the cutting edge and support the tool with your thumb. Rest your wrist and forearm on the work or the bench if you can.

Fig 4.3 Never drive a gouge so deeply into the wood that the corners of the blade sink beneath the surface. If you do, the wood will split.

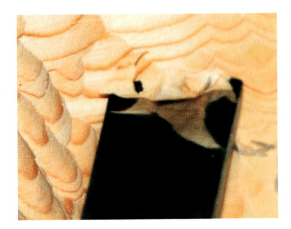

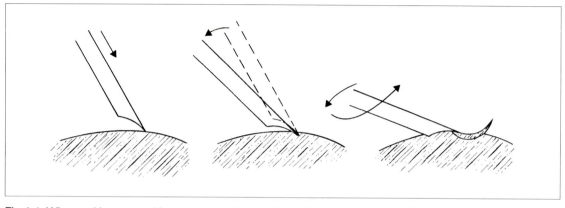

Fig 4.4 When making a cut with a gouge, hold the tool at quite a steep angle and drive the blade into the wood by tapping smartly with the mallet. Lower the gouge handle a little and continue tapping with the mallet. Finally, lower the handle more to scoop out a clean chip.

flying all over the place (see Fig 4.4).

Aim to make chips of even depth and similar length. If they vary too much, the force of your mallet blows is inconsistent, or you may not be keeping your gouge hand steady enough. A large heavy gouge will cut deep wide grooves and require considerable effort to drive its wide cutting edge through the wood, so if it becomes too tiring, change to a narrower gouge with a shallower curve and take smaller cuts. Watch all the time where you are cutting, co-ordinating the mallet blows on the gouge handle, until eventually you can do this automatically without having to look up from the carving. Try to relax your mallet hand as much as possible, but without losing control of it.

Having cut the first furrow across the wood, begin another adjacent to it, which will leave a ridge. Continue working systematically in this way until you have covered the entire area (see Fig 4.5). With experience, you will be able to make long strokes of even depth, allowing you to follow the form of the carving and create a

flow around the shape. As you work down and around the shape, clear away the wood in front first, as this will prevent uncontrolled splitting.

If you find that the mallet slips off the gouge handle as you tap, this may be because its head is too bulbous for the contact area offered. This is likely to occur when carving hard, shiny woods, such as yew or apple. You may also find it difficult to get started, the tool skipping off the surface and not cutting.

Fig 4.5 The initial shaping work with a gouge will leave your carving covered with groups of ridges and furrows.

In this situation, try holding the mallet head in the palm of your hand, which should make it easier to co-ordinate the blows and make contact. You can also use this method if you suffer from tennis elbow, or if the mallet is too heavy for comfort. It may also help to shorten the handle.

If you are right-handed, always work so that you cut from right to left, removing the wood from the vice and turning it around, if necessary, or shifting your own position. This is the more natural movement for a right-handed person, and it will lead to a better shape and a more sweeping action over the carving, as well as being less laborious. Very often, you will find that it is easier to carve one side of the piece than the other for this reason. Obviously, if you are left-handed, the reverse applies.

Never work towards yourself, and keep your hands behind the cutting edge of the tool at all times. Do not blow the chips away; tip them off or use a soft brush, but not your hand because of splinters.

Little by little, work over the whole carving so that you do not remain in one place for too long, otherwise you may lose the proportions of your figure. Keep examining it from all angles, marking the wood that needs removing with a pencil or chalk (see Fig 4.6).

At this stage, your carving will be covered with fairly deep gouge cuts, in groups that flow around the shape. As you work, try to visualize the final figure you are aiming for, which should be fixed clearly in your mind. Compare the shape of the wood with the preliminary drawings that you should have made, as this will help you determine where wood needs removing. The drawings are intended to make you consider your carving from all aspects, and to show you what to remove, not to reveal your drawing talent or provide a scale plan that must be adhered to rigidly.

The next stage is to work over the entire surface with a flatter gouge to remove all the ridges and furrows, and to refine the shape. Cut as before, following the form and shape with shallow cuts. As always, be careful not to dig the corners of the gouge deeply into the wood; the aim is to achieve a smoother surface so that you can see what shape you have. Continue in this way until you have reached the final shape, again comparing your work with the drawings. When the carving feels comfortable in your hands, you will be ready to begin detailing and the more precise hand carving. Final smoothing will be carried out with a scraper.

Fig 4.6 As you work, mark out the areas of wood to be removed with a pencil or piece of chalk.

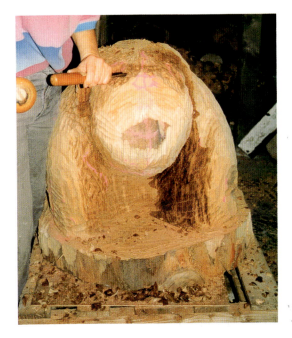

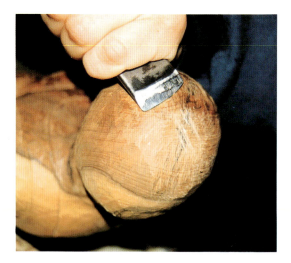

Hand gouge techniques

As your carving progresses, you will need to change from using large deep gouges, for removing excess wood, to small flat gouges for more precise shaping, smoothing and detail work. Most of the time these are applied by hand, or tapped lightly with a mallet, when the force can easily be controlled by placing your index finger behind the head of the mallet as you tap.

A rounded shape, once roughly formed,

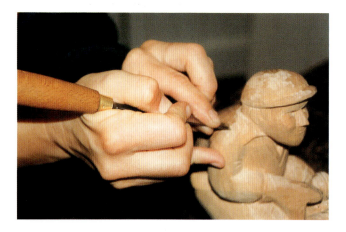

Fig 4.7 You can use a wide no. 3 gouge for smoothing your work instead of a spokeshave. Hold it with the bevel uppermost, applying pressure to the blade with the palm of your left hand. Push the tool forwards with your right, moving the handle at the same time to produce a diagonal slicing movement of the cutting edge.

can be smoothed with a wide no. 3 (Swiss no. 2) gouge, turned bevel uppermost. This method can be used instead of employing a spokeshave if you do not have one.

With the palm of your left hand lying across the back of the blade, just behind the cutting edge, and your right hand pushing the handle, slide the cutting edge forward, at the same time slicing sideways to use the width of the cutting edge. Maintain pressure on the blade and carving with your left hand, guiding the tool around the shape with your right (see Fig 4.7). Take care not to score the wood with the corners of the gouge by applying uneven pressure. The wider the gouge, the easier it will be to slice and cut simultaneously. Do not use a gouge with a greater curve than a no. 3 (Swiss no. 2), or the corners will dig in. A flat chisel can be used in this way but will tend to leave flat facets and will be difficult to guide around the shape.

When carving fine detail, such as an eye, you will have to remove tiny shavings from around it to make it stand out, and to blend in the background. The best tool for this would be a ¼ or ³⁄₁₆in (6 or 8mm) no. 3 gouge, used bevel down (see Fig 4.8).

Fig 4.8 When carving fine detail, hold the blade of the tool in both hands, using your fingers and thumbs as if you are holding a pen. By pushing and twisting with your right hand and resisting that movement with your left, you will gain good control over the tool. This can be improved further by resting your little fingers on the work.

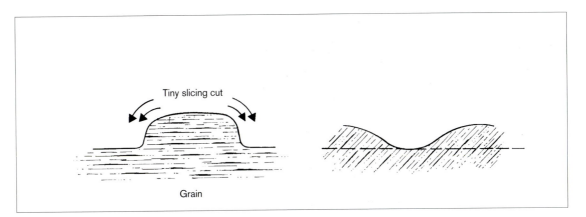

Tiny slicing cut

Grain

Fig 4.9 When finishing your carving, hold the gouge bevel down and use a paring action to slice off tiny chips. This technique is ideal when working around a feature such as an eye, or for removing hollows by paring away the high spots around them. To round over edges on features such as buttons, eyes and feathers, use the gouge bevel uppermost.

In this situation, hold the tool between the fingers of your right hand, about two-thirds of the way down the blade, as if it is a pen. Grip the blade in the same manner with your other hand, but just behind the cutting edge. Rest both little fingers on the work for stability.

Make a slicing cut with the gouge, pushing it forwards and sideways simultaneously, using the full width of the cutting edge. Push with your right hand, but restrain and guide the gouge with your left. In this way, the tiniest of shavings can be removed under complete control.

Practise this technique, as it is very useful and will enable you to make fine adjustments to your carvings with confidence. Blemishes and scratches can also be pared out easily like this. If you hold the gouge in the same manner, but with the bevel uppermost, you can use it to round off edges in confined spaces, or to soften the edges of a channel, when carving primary feathers on a bird, for example (see Fig 4.9).

Never lever or twist away the wood you are removing, as this will break the cutting edge and the tool will need re-grinding. If you find that your tools break along the cutting edges, consider the way in which you use them; you may have fallen into the bad habit of driving the gouge into the wood and twisting it outwards as you remove the chips in a heavy-handed manner. Instead, cut into the wood with the tool, push the blade along, then out to produce a clean entry and exit. Do not dig the corners of the blade into the wood so deeply that they become buried; the wood will split and the tool may become embedded. If this does happen, gently move it from side to side to extract it. Forcing it out will break the blade, as will levering it back and forth. If you are unable to release the tool, take another gouge and very carefully cut away the wood from around it. U-shaped gouges are particularly prone to breaking if misused in this manner.

V tools

The V tool has many uses, but because it has two cutting blades, it must be used carefully and with plenty of forethought. Unless you are using it to cut into end grain, one of the blades may tear into the line you are cutting if this is curved.

As the tool's name implies, it cuts a V-shaped channel, as shown in Fig 4.10, which is used for the initial marking out of a relief design, or detail on a figure, such as ears, eyes, buttons, etc. These are simply relief carvings on a rounded surface. The tool is useful for texturing as well.

To begin with, a V tool can be difficult to use. The aim is to produce a uniformly-sized wood chip that emerges from the centre of the two blades, without stopping cutting until necessary. Work without rocking the tool from side to side, while tapping it steadily with your mallet. The latter will provide better control of the tool, as if used by hand, it may slip and score your work.

Hold the V tool well down its blade, placing your thumb along the underside to support it; rest your elbow on the bench for stability. As with a gouge, always cut from right to left if you are right-handed.

The groove must be of even depth and width, the size of the chip being a useful guide. If it varies in width, you are altering the depth of cut by moving the tool handle up and down as you cut. If it skids off the surface or will not cut, you are probably holding the tool at too shallow an angle. If it still will not cut after raising the handle, examine the blades as described in Chapter 2.

Fig 4.10 A V tool cuts a V-shaped groove that will outline a relief design or mark out detail on a figure in the round. It is also suitable for texturing. It is best used with a mallet. Hold the tool well down the blade, supporting it from below with your thumb; rest your hand and forearm on the bench for stability.

Do not remove the blade from the groove until absolutely necessary. If the chip of wood gets in the way, break it off using your mallet hand, without moving the tool from its position on your work, as it will not be easy to continue cutting in exactly the same place.

Unless the tool is razor sharp, it will tear when cutting across the grain, which is why a V tool should not be used for lettering. If you need to cut a channel across the grain, or if you are trying to cut a narrow projection, such as a plant stalk, use a suitably-shaped gouge (invariably a no. 3, or Swiss no. 2) and cut in from each side.

Although the V tool will cut very well along the grain and in end grain, few designs will require these cuts exclusively. Usually, the line being cut will curve one way or the other, and you will have to make two cuts from opposite directions to prevent the tool from tearing the edge of the design

Fig 4.11 When you cut a curve across the grain with a V tool, one blade will cut cleanly, while the other will tear the wood. Always cut in the direction that will place the tearing on the waste side of the line.

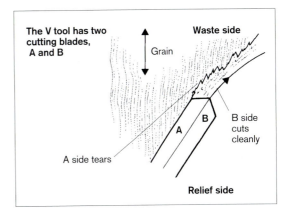

(see Fig 4.11). Determine the direction in which the grain runs and mark arrows on the curved line to indicate the direction to cut so that any tearing of the wood will occur on the waste side of the line – that is, the background of a relief (see Fig 4.12). Practise on some scrap wood first until you can cut two V-grooves that meet each other and have the same depth and width.

When cutting in end grain, these problems do not arise, as the tool lifts out the fibres, leaving a clean channel. The little hook that develops at the point where the two blades meet actually helps this, so I do not to remove it.

As with a gouge, begin cutting with a smart tap of the mallet on the handle, then lower your gouge hand while driving the tool along (see Fig 4.13). Do not cut any deeper than about one third of the width of the tool, and never so that the blades sink completely beneath the surface of the wood.

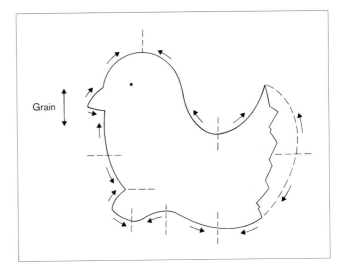

Fig 4.12 When outlining a relief, watch the grain continuously, changing the direction of cut as necessary. Loop generously around narrow projections. If cross-grained, they will break if you attempt to outline them with the V tool. Refine them later with gouges.

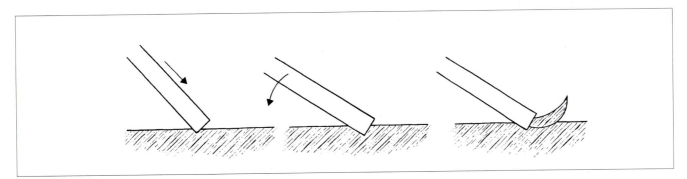

Fig 4.13 When starting a cut with a V tool, hold the tool at a steep angle and tap it smartly with the mallet so that the blade penetrates the wood. Lower the handle slightly and continue tapping, but do not rush. If you lower the handle too much, the tool will skip off the wood, and you may be left with little more than a scratch in the surface. Keep driving the tool until you need to change the direction of cut; if the chip produced obscures the line you are cutting, break it off, but do not lift the tool from its groove.

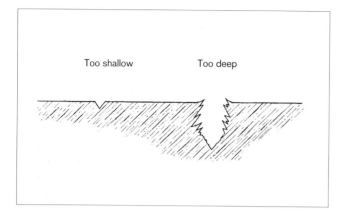

Too shallow   Too deep

Fig 4.14 It is essential to hold the V tool so that it produces a symmetrical groove of even depth and width that does not waver in direction. The deeper you cut, the wider the channel. If you veer to one side or twist the tool, the groove will be lop-sided. If you hold the tool at too shallow an angle, there will hardly be any groove at all, while if you drive it in too deeply, the wood will be split by the corners of the blade.

Fig 4.15 Use a Surform like a cheese grater, holding it with both hands. Push forwards and slightly to the side in one movement, turning it to follow the shape of your carving.

If you do, the wood will split and run ahead of the tool. Maintain an even depth of cut and do not twist the tool from side to side, otherwise you will produce a groove with wavy sides (see Fig 4.14). Take care when cutting along a curved line that you do not tilt the tool, as the groove will not have an even shape and one blade may even dig into the wood.

If the tool tends to slew from one side to the other when cutting, producing an uneven-sided groove, examine the blades end on to determine whether they are symmetrical.

Surforms

A Surform acts in a similar manner to a cheese grater and should be used with the same action. With your work secured firmly, grasp the Surform with both hands, one on the handle and the other on the front of the tool. Push it forwards and slightly sideways in one movement, turning it at the same time to follow the shape of your carving (see Fig 4.15). A convex blade will be easier to use than a flat one, as it can be rolled around the shape more easily. Do not

press hard, as the teeth will dig in and the tool will become immovable.

The Surform usually leaves an ugly scored surface, which will need cleaning up with a spokeshave or a no. 3 gouge. However, it does remove wood quickly. In many cases, it can be used instead of a spokeshave, and it is particularly useful in the hands of the less dextrous.

If you fit the tool with a flat blade, you can use it instead of a plane for levelling the base of a carving. Rub the blade back and forth over any high spots that make the carving unstable. To reveal these, lay a piece of carbon paper on a perfectly flat surface, carbon side up, then stand the carving on the paper and press down. Work the tool from the edges of the base towards the centre, preventing the edges from being broken away.

Spokeshaves

Although some may find a spokeshave difficult to use at first, the tool is worth persevering with. If sharp and correctly set, it will remove fine shavings from your carving, allowing you to adjust its shape and leave a clean surface. Choose a convex-soled spokeshave, rather than one with a flat sole, as you will find it easier to move over your work. You can use it with a pushing or pulling action, but make sure its blade is set straight so that a corner cannot dig in and score the surface.

Holding both handles, rest your thumbs in the hollows or thumb rests and spread your fingers along the handles. Rest the sole on your work and tilt the tool forwards slightly, so that the blade will just bite into the wood as you push it forwards. Lightly push the tool away from you and slightly to one side, so that the blade cuts with a slicing action across its full width, as shown in Fig 4.16. This will produce the cleanest cut. One hand should travel in advance of the other, your thumbs propelling the tool forwards, while your fingers guide it around the wood. Maintain a constant pressure throughout the cut.

When the tool has travelled far enough for the blade to have sliced across its full width, complete the stroke by drawing it back, keeping the sole against the wood so

Fig 4.16 Hold a spokeshave with both hands, tilting it so that the blade bites into the wood. Then push it away from you so that the blade cuts with a slicing action.

that the tool is kept at the same slight angle. By raising or dropping either hand while moving the tool back and forth, you can round and shape the carving.

If you cannot make the tool cut, make sure that the blade is projecting far enough from the sole. If the spokeshave is held at too shallow or too steep an angle, it will not cut. With practice, however, holding it at the correct angle will become automatic.

If the spokeshave cuts, but you find it extremely hard work, try reducing the projection of the blade. The bevel length may be too short, in which case, it should be re-ground to a longer length. Also, make sure the sole is smooth and shiny, otherwise you will have to overcome extra friction when cutting. If necessary, retract the blade and polish the sole using the side of your slipstone followed by metal polishing paste.

If the tool chatters and leaves little ridges in your work, it may be because you are not

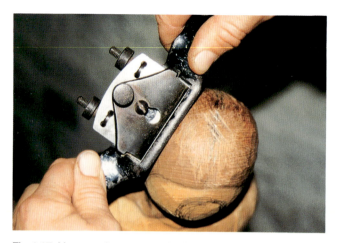

Fig 4.17 You can also use a spokeshave by pulling it towards you.

maintaining a constant pressure on the tool as it cuts, or not using a slicing action, or the blade may project too far from the sole. To improve the slicing action, move your leading hand further forwards when you push, but in doing so, make sure you do not lift the sole from the wood.

When pulling the tool towards you, the same slicing action is required, using the full width of the blade. Tilt the tool towards you as you pull, achieving the shape you want by raising or dropping one hand or the other (see Fig 4.17).

Planes

The main purpose of a plane when carving is to level the base of your work or to prepare a board for relief carving (see Fig 4.18). Before using it, make sure that the blade is set horizontally within the mouth and that it projects sufficiently to make a fine cut. Stand directly in line with the wood and hold the plane square to it, pressing down on the front knob when starting the stroke, and on the handle at the end of the stroke. Always work in the direction of the grain, unless you are planing end grain, and at the end of each stroke, take care not to let the plane tilt over the edge of the wood or drag it back towards you. Simply lift it from the surface.

Fig 4.18 When preparing a board for a relief carving, plane it in the direction of the grain. Lift the plane from the wood after each stroke; do not let it tilt over the end of the board or drag it back towards you.

When planing end grain, adjust the blade so that it takes a very fine cut, and work from the edges in towards the centre so that the edges do not break away. When levelling the base of a carving, mark the high spots and remove them as described for a Surform.

The cabinet maker's scraper

The scraper is normally held in both hands and used with a pushing action in the direction of the grain. Its purpose is to minutely adjust a shape and remove any irregularities in the surface before adding any texturing or detail to the carving. Never use a piece of broken glass as a substitute.

Rest one of the long edges on the surface, holding the two short sides low down between your thumbs and fingers, as shown in Fig 4.19. Steady the scraper by resting your little fingers on the work. Tilt the

upper edge of the tool away from you until you feel the lower edge biting into the surface. Maintaining that angle, push the tool away from you, keeping an even pressure, until you reach the end of the stroke. Lift the tool at this point, as if you are stroking the carving, then gently place it back on the wood and begin the next stroke. Take care not to drag the scraper back towards you at the end of the stroke, as you will be working against the grain and undoing all your good work. This will also dull the cutting edge rapidly.

Work methodically over the surface in this manner, removing all scratches, dimples and other blemishes. A sharp scraper should produce tiny curls of wood, not dust. When the edge becomes dull, turn the tool around and use the other burr on that edge, followed by the two burrs on the other edge.

If the wood is coarse grained, such as ash or oak, corrugations may appear because of the difference in hardness of the annual rings. In this situation, work across the wood at a slight angle so that the scraper cuts diagonally across the fibres. This will produce a more even cut.

If used with the grain, the scraper should produce a shiny surface, but if used against it, the result will be a dull surface. This is particularly noticeable when scraping the end grain of a convex shape, such as the top of a head. In this case, scrape towards the highest

Fig 4.19 Hold a scraper close to the bottom edge between your fingers and thumbs, resting your hands on the workpiece or the bench for stability. Rounding off the corners of the scraper with a file or grindstone will prevent them from digging into the wood.

Fig 4.20 When scraping end grain, always work from the edges to the centre. If you are working on a curved surface, such as the top of a head, scrape towards the summit from all sides. If you scrape 'downhill', you will produce a dull woolly looking surface and may even lift out tufts of wood.

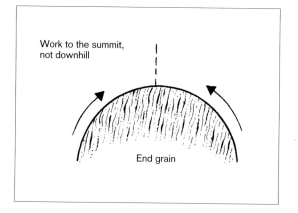

point, from all directions, as shown in Fig 4.20.

In a confined space, such as where two surfaces meet at a narrow angle, the scraper can be used in another way. Hold it so that the upper edge leans towards you and push it away from you as before. This will bring the lower cutting edge into play. As before, lift the scraper at the end of each stroke and take care not to dig its corners into the wood. To prevent this from happening, round them over with a file or grindstone.

You can also use a skew chisel as a scraper, which is particularly useful in a confined space. However, the cutting edge needs to be at quite a sharp angle (about 45°) to reach into narrow gaps. Hold the tool as if it is a pen and scrape sideways with the cutting edge. Take care not to dig the point of the blade into the surface. You will find a short chisel much easier to use in this manner than a long one.

If the wood has interlocked grain, a normal cabinet scraper will be too wide to use effectively, since it will overlap the various stripes, cutting against the grain at some points and with it at others. In this situation, use the end of a small no. 3 gouge, holding the tool like a pen and scraping each stripe of grain separately in the correct direction. This is a tedious chore when working on a large area and is the reason why this type of wood should be avoided if possible.

This method will have to be used if you come across patches of grain that run contrary

to the normal direction within the piece, which is common in yew. Small confined spaces, or surfaces around details such as eyes, can also be scraped effectively using a no. 3 gouge. The ¼in (6mm) width is the most versatile.

Never use a gouge with a greater sweep than a no. 3 (Swiss no. 2) for scraping, as the corners may dig into your work. For the same reason, care should be taken when using a straight or skew chisel for scraping.

Using abrasives

You should use abrasives sparingly in woodcarving, as in some cases they can actually spoil your work. They are best reserved for finishing large areas, or for smooth, close-grained carvings that will be handled frequently.

The sharpness of a detailed figure carving will be lost if it is rubbed down with abrasive paper, and the piece will lack character and life. For the same reason, most relief carvings should not be smoothed with abrasives. In addition, edged tools should not be used on an abraded surface, as they will soon become dull due to minute abrasive particles remaining on the wood.

There are many types of abrasive paper,

often simply and incorrectly referred to as sandpaper, which are graded by the degree of abrasion they offer: the higher the grit number, the finer the paper. Using too coarse a paper will leave scratch marks on the surface of the wood. Always buy the best quality, as cheap paper sheds its particles and does not last. I usually recommend garnet paper, which is made from crushed crystals of garnet, heat treated to increase their hardness. In use, the crystals fracture in parallel horizontal planes, thus forming fresh cutting edges. These act like tiny scrapers (unlike the particles of ordinary glasspaper, which fracture to leave sharp points that will scratch the surface). Garnet paper can be bought from a good ironmonger's shop, and is available in grits from 120 (coarse) to 320 (very fine).

The quality of the final finish of your carving will depend on the preparation work carried out before using an abrasive. For example, the latter can never be a substitute for the meticulous tidying up of edges that meet or smoothing of surfaces with a scraper, both of which are quite lengthy procedures. If either is omitted, you will produce a carving that is second rate, and the abrasives will simply deepen all the hollows and dimples, leaving a flawed and irregular surface.

Where a flat surface needs abrading, such as the border of a relief panel, wrap the paper around a flat piece of wood or cork sanding block and rub only in the direction of the grain. Begin with a coarse paper and follow with finer grades until the surface is completely smooth, tapping the block frequently to dislodge dust from the paper. Then, before the final abrading, wipe the surface with a damp cloth to remove abrasive dust and raise the grain of the wood as the fibres swell slightly in reaction to the moisture. The final rub will then produce a very smooth surface. If the end grain of a relief carving need abrading, work from the edges towards the centre, as when planing, to avoid rounding the corners.

In confined areas, emery boards can be used. Alternatively, abrasive paper can be fastened to a spatula, tongue depressor, plastic knitting needle or any other pliable material, using double-sided adhesive tape. When tidying up edges that meet, fold the paper around the edge of a spatula.

Abrading the inside of a bowl is easiest if the paper is wrapped around a piece of sponge. This method is also useful when working on very soft wood that cannot be scraped cleanly without lifting shreds, usually because it is nearly rotten (see Fig 4.21). In this case, abrading the surface is the answer. Take care, however, not to round any sharp

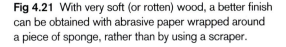

Fig 4.21 With very soft (or rotten) wood, a better finish can be obtained with abrasive paper wrapped around a piece of sponge, rather than by using a scraper.

edges. When doing this, always wear a dust mask, as such woods are noxious.

Finishing your carving

A pleasant and easily applied finish for a carving is a good-quality colourless wax polish, buffed to a good sheen with a soft brush or lint-free duster. Such a finish will emphasize the grain pattern and colour of the wood without the need for messy brushes or spirit-based sealers. Although the latter are advocated by some carvers, I have never found them to offer any particular advantage. You can also use a wax polish immediately you have completed your carving, without having to abrade between coats of a sealer, or wait for long periods while each coat dries. You need not worry about dust adhering to the surface, either.

A carving in a blandly coloured wood such as lime, can be enhanced considerably by applying Danish oil. This is available from all good DIY shops and ironmongers, and should be shaken well, applied with a brush, and allowed to dry overnight. The carving should then be waxed.

When you are happy that your carving has been finished to the best of your ability, apply a coat of cheap colourless and silicone-free wax polish, using your fingertips so that you can check that the work is completely smooth. An old toothbrush can be used to apply the wax to textured surfaces and fine detail. If necessary, bend the handle after immersing it in hot water so that you can reach into confined spaces. Leave the polish

for a few minutes so that it is absorbed by the wood, after which time any remaining imperfections in your work will be clearly visible. Remove these by careful paring and scraping, then apply more wax and check again.

If your carving will be handled frequently and you want a very smooth finish, rub the waxed surfaces with 320 grit garnet paper or very fine flour paper. The wax will mix with the fine dust produced, leaving a smooth silky finish. Any surface cracks will also be filled with the mixture. Finally, buff the carving with a duster and apply further coats of a good-quality polish, not a cream or spray. Leave each coat to soak into the wood overnight before polishing with a duster. Handle the carving as much as possible to produce a patina.

If the wax clogs any texturing or fine detail, pick it out with a wooden cocktail stick, or brush it out with an old hard toothbrush. A carving made grubby through handling can be scrubbed clean with a nailbrush, soap and lukewarm water. Then it should be scraped, abraded and re-waxed. Do not worry about going back to the piece or adjusting any part of it, even after several years, as newly cut surfaces will soon darken and blend in with the rest.

When beginning a carving, it is always best to use a wood of an appropriate colour, rather than attempt to change its colour by staining. The stain will show up any flaws, so you cannot disguise a poor surface finish with it, while the effect is likely to be patchy where the end grain pores absorb more. If you do need to colour the wood, however, spirit-based felt pens are very effective and will polish up to a very fine shine.

The underside of a carving in the round should always be finished by gluing felt to it; do not use self-adhesive baize, as it gradually peels off and looks shoddy. Place the carving on the felt and draw around the base, cutting the piece out with sharp scissors. Score the base of the carving with a skew chisel or knife and apply PVA woodworking adhesive. Place the felt on the glued surface and press outwards from the centre, wiping off any excess glue. The felt will stretch a little, but this can be trimmed off when the glue has dried

Carvings that will be placed outdoors need a finish that will withstand the weather. Raw linseed oil is especially good for oak, though there are other types, such as teak oil. Oil finishes usually need to be re-applied each year. Another suitable finish for outdoor items is a proprietary brand of polyurethane marine varnish. Clear cellulose spray can be used both indoors and out. It gives a pleasant finish, particularly on light coloured woods. An alternative finish for exterior use is a silicone-based wax or car polish, which will repel moisture. It should be applied a couple of times a year.

A bowl or platter intended for use with food can be finished by rubbing it with medicinal liquid paraffin, which is odourless, colourless and tasteless. Various other edible oils can also be used, but some may become tainted in time, and the bowl may need scrubbing and re-scraping before a fresh application.

Chapter 5

Health & Safety

Normal workshop safety procedures apply when carving, but particular attention should be paid to the following:

- Never rush or work when you are tired, as this is just the time when accidents are likely to happen.
- Do not allow your bench to become cluttered; leave only the tools that you are using and store the rest until you need them. Make sure you have enough room to move freely around the bench.
- Secure the carving so that it cannot slip or move as you cut; never carve with it in your hand or in your lap.
- Sharpen your tools frequently, and always before a carving session. Dull tools require more effort to make them cut, making your carving tedious and unnecessarily laborious.
- Never cut towards yourself; turn your work or change your position so that you always cut from right to left, if right-handed, and vice versa. Cutting in an unnatural direction will be arduous and tiresome, and is usually unnecessary.
- Keep both hands well behind the cutting edge of your tool at all times; never carve one-handed.
- Never apply a levering action to your tools, as they will break.
- Do not use a mallet with any tool that has

a bent blade. The tool will be uncontrollable and the blade may break. These are hand tools only.

- Never use your hand instead of a mallet.
- If you drop a tool, do not try to catch it, but move smartly out of the way.
- Clear the shavings and chips from your work with a brush, not your hand, as this will protect you from splinters. Do not blow them away either, especially when carving a hollow, as the chips may fly up into your eyes. Sweep up sawdust as soon as possible. It will make the floor slippery, while some types, such as yew, are irritants and should not be breathed in.
- When using a grindstone, always wear protective goggles, not spectacles. Do not rely on the eye shields fitted to the machine, as these are inadequate. Remember that the blade of the tool will become very hot when grinding, so do not handle it; dip it in water frequently to prevent drawing its temper.

Holding your carving safely

Your carving must be held securely while you are working on it, otherwise accidents can happen. It is very irritating and frustrating if the piece moves or slips at a crucial moment.

Ideally, you should have a sturdy woodworking bench that will not rock or slide when in use. This should be fitted with a quick-release vice that will open to 15in (381mm) or more. The vice jaws should have wooden face plates with the grain running vertically, otherwise they will split when tightened around a large piece of wood. The screws securing the face plates must be countersunk to prevent them from damaging your carving, while the vice screw should have a thread guard, not only to protect your work, but also to prevent chips and dust entering the mechanism. Clean the latter regularly and keep it lubricated, together with the slide bars, using a silicone spray, such as WD40.

If the vice has no screw guard, wrap your work in a thick cloth or sponge to prevent the screw from damaging it. Alternatively, place a piece of scrap wood between the screw and the work.

A sturdy table makes a good alternative to a bench, particularly if it has an overlapping top, as this will allow you to secure your work with cramps. If the table is old and the surface unimportant, you may be able to make a cradle for your work, as shown in Fig 5.1. Nail lengths of wood to the top around the carving, leaving enough space to insert two wooden wedges, which will hold it tightly in place. The wedges should be fitted rough faces together so that they do not slip, but if your mallet blows do jar them loose, coat the faces with a rubber-based glue, such as Cow Gum or Copydex. Allow this to dry,

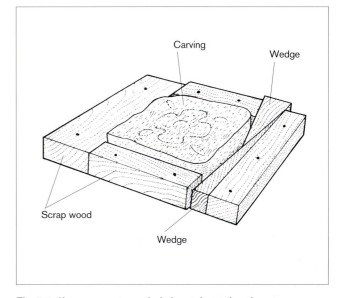

Fig 5.1 If you are not worried about damaging the surface you are working on, you can make a cradle to hold your carving securely. Nail or screw lengths of wood around it, leaving space for one or two wedges. For added stability, rest the carving on a damp cloth.

then fit the wedges together. To prevent the carving from jumping out of the cradle, you may be able place a long lath over the top and secure this to the edges of the table with cramps.

G-cramps can also be used to hold your work to the bench or table top, particularly if it is a relief carving. Always place a piece of scrap wood between the carving and the cramp head. This will distribute the pressure from the cramp and prevent it from damaging the wood. Fit the cramp so that its main body is beneath the table top, otherwise this will be in the way and may even injure your face or head as you lean over your work.

The reach of a G-cramp can be extended by placing a long lath across the work, as

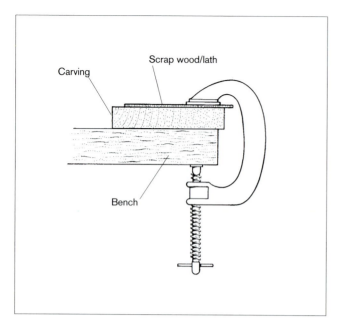

Carving

Scrap wood/lath

Bench

Fig 5.2 You can extend the reach of G-cramps by placing a lath across the top of your work and clamping it down at the ends. Always place a piece of scrap wood beneath the cramp head to protect your work, and fit the cramp so that the main body is below the bench top and out of the way.

shown in Fig 5.2. Keep the thread of the cramp clean and lubricated with silicone spray.

If you are unable to leave your bench permanently set up, the folding Black and Decker Workmate bench will be useful. A special device is available to increase its opening capacity, while relief carvings can be held satisfactorily between the plastic pegs provided. If these prove too short, make longer wooden replacements. To improve the stability of this bench, you can weight it down with concrete blocks, or simply place your feet on the base.

When carving small or finely detailed work, carver's chops will prove invaluable. These are a wooden version of the engineer's vice, which are secured to the bench top by a single screw from below (see

Fig 5.3). This allows the device to be swivelled to the ideal position for working. Alternatively, the chops can be held in a vice, attached to a block or clamped to the table edge. A hand rest is incorporated, which is particularly useful when working on very delicate carvings, while the surface area of the jaws can be increased by inserting thick pieces of plywood between them and the work.

Another effective, but less satisfactory, method of securing your work is the carver's screw. This is inserted through a hole in the bench top and into a corresponding hole drilled in the carving (or a piece of scrap wood attached to the base of the carving). It is tightened with a wrench from beneath the bench. Unfortunately, this device is somewhat restricting, since it holds the

Fig 5.3 Carver's chops are ideal for holding small or awkwardly-shaped carvings.

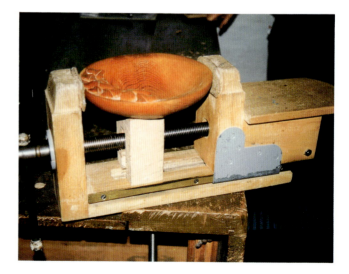

work at a set angle, which may make carving some areas difficult. In addition, you must remember that there is a hole in the centre of the carving that may cause problems when carving deeply.

A ball-and-socket device is available for attaching to the base of a carving and then fastening in a vice to hold it steady (see Fig 5.4). This allows you to turn the carving to a more suitable angle for working, but once fastened, the attachment makes it impossible to handle the carving. Personally, I find this frustrating, since if a carving feels good in your hands, it is usually the 'right' shape. Another drawback is that you can damage your tools if you knock them against its metal surface. It requires substantial securing screws, otherwise the carving will be jarred loose by your mallet blows, and the adjusting lever can also get in the way.

A much simpler method of holding your work in a vice, but clear of its jaws, is to screw a block of wood to the base of the carving and clamp this, as shown in Fig 5.5. If you are working on a very soft piece of wood, you can even glue the block in place. Coat both sides of a piece of paper with glue and place this between the block and the carving. When you have finished the carving, detach the block by inserting a knife blade between the two. The base of the carving and the surface of the block must be absolutely flat, however, otherwise the glue will not hold. Double-sided carpet tape can be used instead.

Another method of securing your work, without drilling or driving screws into it, is

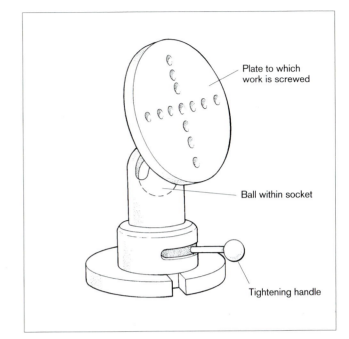

Fig 5.4 This ball-and-socket device can be used to hold your work in a vice and allow it to be pivoted to the best angle for carving. However, it is rather expensive and the adjusting handle can get in the way, and you can damage your tools against the metal.

Fig 5.5 If your carving is too large to fit in a vice, screw a narrow piece of wood to the base and clamp this in the vice instead. If the wood is quite soft, you can glue a block of wood to the base, inserting a sheet of paper between the two, which will ease removal of the block when you have finished. Whether you use screws or glue, make sure that the base of your carving and the mating face of the wooden block are perfectly flat, otherwise the block will not hold.

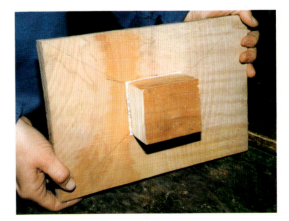

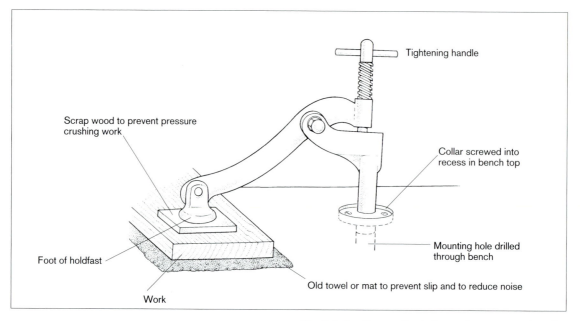

Scrap wood to prevent pressure crushing work

Tightening handle

Collar screwed into recess in bench top

Foot of holdfast

Mounting hole drilled through bench

Old towel or mat to prevent slip and to reduce noise

Work

Fig 5.6 Another method of securing your work to the top of your bench is the holdfast.

the bench holdfast (see Fig 5.6). This makes use of a collar attached to the bench top that can be lowered on to the carving. It is more suitable for securing a relief carving than one in the round, which may swivel unless placed on a damp cloth. Even so, it is easy to knock your head on the device as you lean over your work. As with a G-cramp, scrap wood must be used to protect the carving from damage by the holdfast head.

Manufacturers regularly offer new and updated devices for holding your work. Whichever you choose, make sure it allows you to turn your work easily, release it quickly and hold quite large pieces without restricting you in any way. I use a quick-release bench vice for initial heavy mallet work, and carver's chops for more delicate carving.

Certain types of wood, apple and yew for example, become shiny and slippery when carved. This makes them tend to move as you work. Wrapping a damp cloth around

the carving will help prevent the problem. Chock it underneath so that it cannot move down during carving. In some cases, you may be able to turn the carving so that you are cutting towards the bench, rather than towards the side of the vice. Mounting the work on a squared block and clamping this in the vice will also help, as will attaching fine abrasive paper to the vice jaws with double-sided tape. If all else fails, take smaller shallower cuts, and make sure that your tools are really sharp so that you do not need to apply unnecessary force.

A small relief carving can be held in the vice, but always place a piece of scrap wood beneath it for support and make sure the grain of the carving runs at right angles to the vice jaws. The latter is essential to prevent the carving from cracking as the vice is tightened. Alternatively, fasten it to a flat base using double-sided carpet tape, and fasten the base in the vice.

If you have a bench with a tool-well set in the top, you can place a larger relief carving in the well, resting it on a mat or towel. The edge of the carving should be against the side of the well that you are cutting towards, for example the left if you are right-handed. Pack the remaining well space with wedges and clamp the carving down, protecting it from the cramp heads with scrap wood. If the wood is warped slightly, support it from below so that it cannot bounce as you cut, which may cause it to split (see Fig 5.7). If the wood is quite soft and does not require heavy tool work, you can glue a block of wood to the back and fasten this in the vice instead.

Another method of holding a relief is to set it into a larger board and clamp this to the bench. Mark the outline of the relief on the board, then carefully cut it out with a chisel or router so that the carving is a tight fit in the opening. If you make it too large, you can always pack it out with scraps of wood so that it cannot move. A similar method is to place the carving on a peg board and fasten it tightly with pegs and wedges. A revolving socket attached to the back of the board can be clamped in the vice, allowing you to turn your work when necessary without dislodging the carving. A small light relief can even be placed on the type of non-slip tray mat used by the disabled and available from large

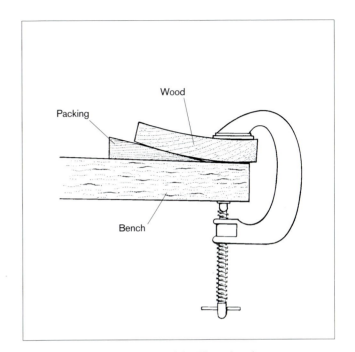

Fig 5.7 If your wood is warped, it will tend to rise when it is clamped to the bench top. In this case, support it from below with scrap wood, otherwise it may bounce and split as you work on it.

chemists, or rested in a sand-filled canvas bag.

A bowl is best held in a vice or carver's chops, supported from underneath by scrap wood, but if it will not fit, it can be held on the bench with G-cramps and a lath that passes over the top of the bowl. If this method is too restricting, however, and your wood is quite soft, the paper, glue and squared block method might be the answer. An alternative is to screw a block to the top of the bowl so that it can be held while you carve the outside, then glue a block to the base for carving the inside.

Part 2
Projects

The 10 projects that follow are designed to teach you carving techniques in a logical, progressive order, and once you have mastered them, you will have acquired the necessary skills to carve anything you like – techniques are the tools of creativity, which is itself limited only by your mind and confidence. Use your imagination for your carvings: don't simply copy someone else's ideas. It is far more challenging and interesting to develop your own style of carving, although you may be inspired by the work of others to do so.

I do not use power tools, machinery or rotary burrs in any of the projects, because I believe it is important to learn all about the wood and its characteristics, and to be competent in the use of handcarving techniques. While there is good reason to use such equipment for the rather onerous task of removing large quantities of waste wood from a large carving, many people cannot afford such tools. Many others would not wish to sit dressed in a mask and goggles, grinding a piece of wood to dust, with all the associated noise, when the same result could be achieved more quietly, cleanly, and in some situations, more quickly, with hand tools.

Before you begin any carving project, it is important to have a clear idea in your mind of exactly what you want to carve, otherwise the results may be unsatisfactory. For this reason, it is helpful to make some preliminary drawings, even if they are not of high artistic standard. They will help concentrate your mind on the project. Precisely copying a pattern designed by someone else can be very restricting, as it does not allow you to study the subject in detail, and you may fail to use the qualities of your piece of wood creatively. Very often, during the course of a carving, inspirations arise that make it possible to make improvements and add features to the original idea you started with. All the projects that follow can be used as a basis for your own carving, altering and adapting it as you wish.

Carvers sometimes have difficulty in finding a subject to carve. However, as you progress with your carving, you will begin to look at the world about you through different eyes, seeing plenty of suitable subjects. If you follow the simple footsteps set out here, you will be able to carve them all with confidence, and you will be surprised at what you can achieve!

Chapter 6

Introduction to Carving in the Round

Hedgehog

I have found this to be an ideal beginner's project. It teaches you how to carve a rounded shape, and how to add detail in the form of features, as well as introducing simple texturing and finishing techniques.

Working with the grain

Before you gain experience in carving, it can be difficult to work out the lie of the wood fibres, the grain, and the correct direction in which to cut. All cuts should be made *with* the grain, and you may need to turn your work to do this so that you do not cut towards yourself. Cuts made in the correct direction will be smooth and shiny. Those made against the grain will be rough and jagged.

For the beginner, it is best to think of the wood fibres as if they were a bundle of pencils, held together with a rubber band. When you sharpen pencils, you always cut outwards and away from them, across the leads at an angle. If each pencil represents a fibre of wood, you will be cutting *with* the grain if you sharpen them in this direction. If you attempt to sharpen them by cutting into the bundle (i.e. *against* the grain), you

Tools you will need

- Your widest, such as a 1in (25mm) no. 3 (Swiss no. 2) gouge
- ½in (13mm) or ⅝in (16mm) no. 9 gouge
- ¼in (6mm) no. 3 (Swiss no. 2) gouge
- ⅛in (3mm) or 3/16in (4mm) 60° V tool
- ¼in (6mm) 60° V tool
- ¼in (6mm) skew chisel
- Surform
- Spokeshave
- Cabinet scraper
- Mallet

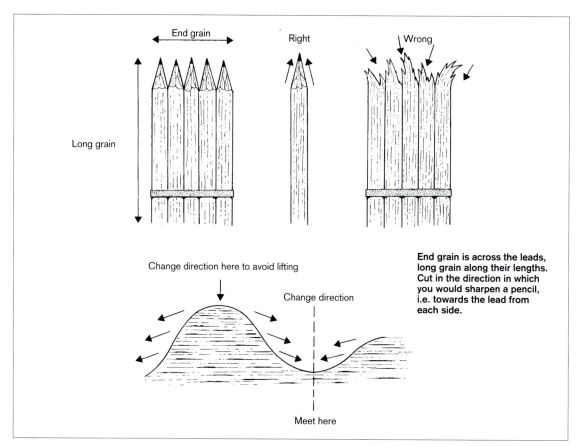

Long grain

End grain

Right

Wrong

Change direction here to avoid lifting

Change direction

Meet here

End grain is across the leads, long grain along their lengths. Cut in the direction in which you would sharpen a pencil, i.e. towards the lead from each side.

Fig 6.1 How to work with the grain.

Choosing and preparing the wood

will scatter and break them away from each other. This is exactly what happens with the wood fibres when you cut in the wrong direction: the tool will dig in and the wood will split and tear.

So when carving, always examine the surface of the wood to determine the correct direction of cut from the way in which the fibres lie. The fibres will be visible as fine lines if they run parallel to the surface, otherwise you will see them as specks or fine dots, which are the ends of the fibres. Always cut outwards and away from their ends and you will be working correctly: *with* the grain (see Fig 6.1)

I used an offcut of mahogany for this project, measuring 7 x 4 x 3in (178 x 102 x 76mm), but you could use any of the woods listed in the glossary on page 175. The wood needs to be straight-grained, so avoid any with interlocking grain. The grain should run lengthwise (from the nose to the tail of the hedgehog), not across. Alternatively, you could use a half-round log, but if you do, you need to consider the amount of curvature. It must be curved symmetrically along its length. Choose a complete, unsplit log, which is straight-grained and free of knots, and cut the ends so that they are parallel to each other. Then fasten it in your vice and remove the bark. If this proves obstinate, use your widest gouge and chip it free, working along the grain. This done, look at the log end-on, choose the more symmetrical half, and split it down the middle with an axe. Then flatten the base, using a Surform or a mallet and a wide no. 3 gouge. Remove any humps, then plane the surface smooth, working from the centre towards each end.

Fig 6.2 Transfer the top, side, front and back profiles of the hedgehog to your block of wood.

Preliminary sketches

The first stage of any carving is to make preliminary sketches of the finished piece. These do not have to be particularly artistic; their function is to clarify the basic design in your mind and help you think in three dimensions. All you need is a rough outline, showing where the excess wood needs to be removed first. With experience, some carvers bypass the sketch stage, but for the time being regard it as an essential element in producing a successful carving.

Transfer your drawings to the wood, as shown in Fig 6.2. Draw the top, the sides and the end outlines on the wood, using chalk, and mark which side is top. Make the outlines fill as much of the wood as possible, which will minimize the amount of wood you will need to remove. Try to prevent the outline from becoming squashed or out of proportion. Finally, draw in the centre-line, from the nose to the rear end.

Shaping the rear end

First mark the centre-point of the rear end. Since the end will be rounded, this represents the farthest projecting point (see Fig 6.3). Place the cutting edge of the ⅝in (16mm) or the ½in (13mm) no. 9 gouge about ¾in (19mm) from the end of the wood on the top corner, so that you are cutting *outwards* and *with* the grain. Give the gouge a sharp tap with the mallet, but do not be so heavy-handed that the corners of the gouge sink beneath the surface of the wood. Now drop your gouge hand slightly and tap again with the mallet, continuing to cut until you almost reach the edge of the wood. At this point, prevent the blade from shooting off the end by

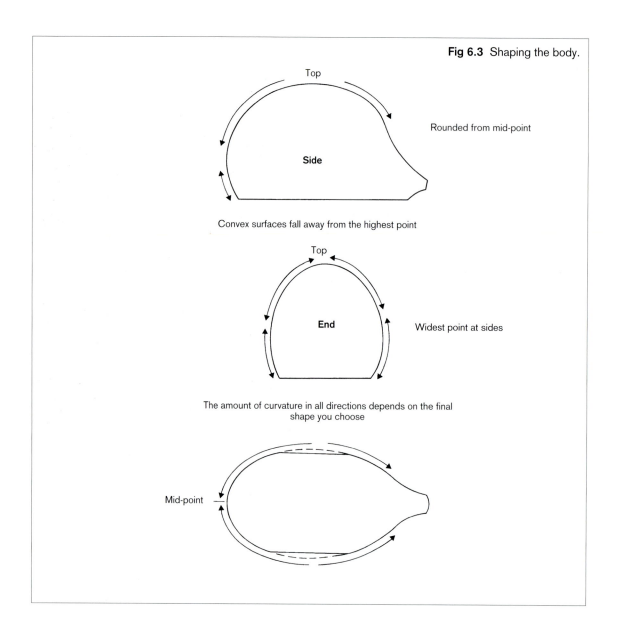

Fig 6.3 Shaping the body.

Top

Side

Rounded from mid-point

Convex surfaces fall away from the highest point

Top

End

Widest point at sides

The amount of curvature in all directions depends on the final
shape you choose

Mid-point

gradually raising your gouge hand as you approach the edge, guiding the cut *over* and *around* the edge, at the same time aiming the tool towards the centre mark. In this way, you will cut off the sharp angle without the risk of splitting the wood. Start with a short cut, and if you find the wood swivels as you cut, turn the block so that you are cutting towards the bench, rather than parallel to it.

Now begin your second cut, a little deeper and a little further back, but in the same furrow, finishing nearer the centre mark than before. Work a row of cuts in this way, starting from alternate sides of the second cut. Remove an equal amount of wood from each side, and continuing to aim for the centre mark with each stroke

Fig 6.4 (left) Removing the corners of the rear end.

Fig 6.5 (below) The roughly rounded rear end.

Fig 6.6 The rear end must be shaped symmetrically.

(as shown in Fig 6.4). Go on to the upper corners, then the lower corners, removing them in the same manner.

Next, begin another set of cuts at each corner, about halfway along the previous rows, close to the edge of the wood. Cut deeper and steeper, still heading for the centre mark, so that the gouge cuts into the remaining flat surface with steep, short cuts. This process removes the sharp edges left by the previous set of cuts. Make longer strokes at the corners, shorter ones as you move across the width, and then lengthen them again as you reach the next corner. Continue until you have roughly shaped the whole end surface up to the centre mark (see Fig 6.5).

Draw a mid-way line around the middle of the hedgehog. Because the upper surface will be more rounded than the lower, the upper corners need to be rounded off as far back as this line. Twist the gouge slightly as

you work, so that it cuts around and over the corners while still moving outwards, with the grain, towards the centre-line. The rounded end needs to be symmetrical, so remove the carving from the vice and re-draw the centre-line so that it passes through the centre mark. Mark the wood that needs removing with chalk, replace the carving in the vice, and pare away the waste, little by little, using shallow cuts. Keep working towards the centre mark, across the bottom as well as the top and sides, until the shape is symmetrical (see Fig 6.6). This process may take longer than

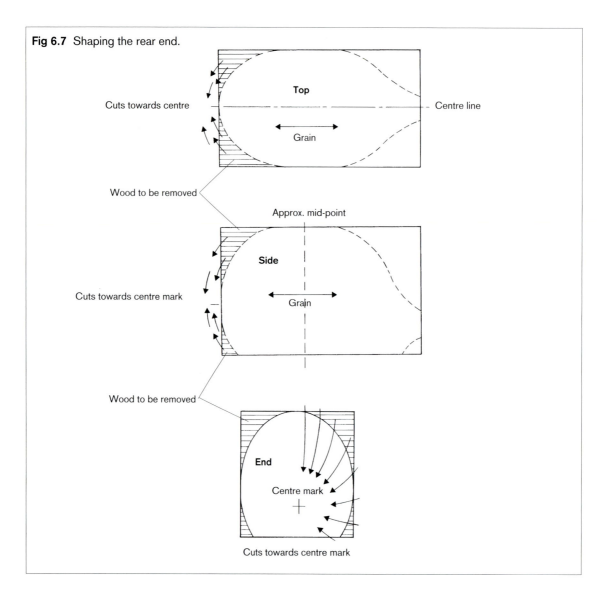

Fig 6.7 Shaping the rear end.

you expect, but work carefully and methodically, as the symmetry is vital if your hedgehog is to look right (see Fig 6.7).

You will find it harder to cut across the end grain, because you are cutting across the ends of the wood fibres. Sharp carving tools are essential when cutting these areas, and if you notice little tufts of wood adhering to the cutting edge of your gouge, or see a score mark in the same place each time you make a cut, sharpen the gouge immediately.

Shaping the head

Mark the centre of the nose, quite low down, on the centre-line that runs down the flat end of the block or log. The face will be cone-like in shape, and the wood will need removing in a similar manner to sharpening a pencil.

Begin in the same way as when shaping the rear end, placing the gouge about ¾in (19mm) back from the top corner. Hold the gouge at a fairly steep angle, driving it along and outwards with the mallet to cut off the corner (as shown in Fig 6.8). Again, work with the grain.

Make the next cut adjacent to the first, still aiming the gouge towards the tip of the nose. Then make another cut in the same manner on the other side of the first cut. As the tip of the blade approaches the edge of the wood, do not lift your gouge hand, as you did when rounding the rear end, but keep each cut directed at the tip of the nose (see Fig 6.9). Continue in this way, all around the log, making longer cuts around the top and

Fig 6.8 Removing the corners at the front of the hedgehog.

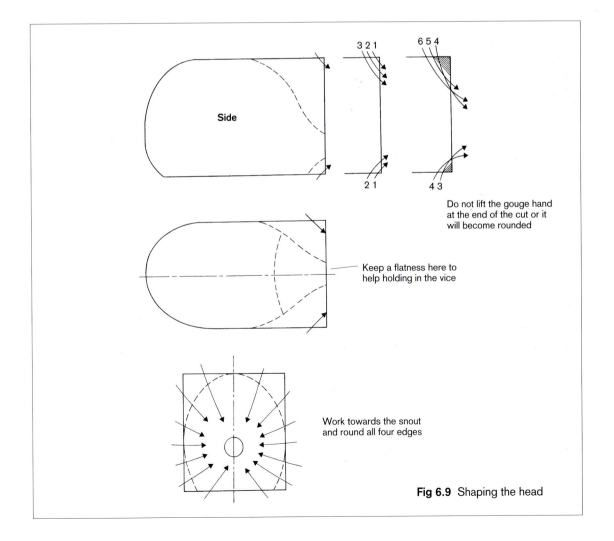

Do not lift the gouge hand at the end of the cut or it will become rounded

Keep a flatness here to help holding in the vice

Work towards the snout and round all four edges

Fig 6.9 Shaping the head

shorter ones at the bottom, so that the snout begins to slope downwards and takes on a lop-sided conical shape. Increase the length of your cuts by starting successive rows further back along the wood, and overlap the previous cuts so that they finish progressively nearer the tip of the nose.

Leave a small flat area, about ¼in (6mm) square, on the actual tip of the nose so that the hedgehog can be held lengthways in the vice.

At the corners, work around from the sides, bringing the snout tidily into the body. If the snout becomes too short and stubby,

Fig 6.10 Begin refining the snout with clockwise curving cuts.

Fig 6.11 Complete the rounding of the snout with anti-clockwise cuts.

lengthen it by removing more wood from the upper corners to make the face fall further back into the body. If it becomes too wide for its length, remove an equal amount of wood from each side of the body by cutting outwards from the tip of the nose, lengthening and overlapping successive cuts until the mid-way line on each side is reached. Then turn the hedgehog around and repeat the process, cutting outwards from the rear end to the mid-way line. As you reach the latter, take extra care and make shallow cuts, as it is very easy to lift and split off a piece if you cut too deeply from the wrong side of the line. If this happens, carefully pare back the surface to the depth of the split, and adjust the other side of the body to match.

Having obtained the basic shape of the snout, refine it by rounding it laterally, making anti-clockwise spiral cuts along and towards the tip of the nose, and working slightly across the grain (see Fig 6.10). Work all around the face, beginning your cuts near the tip and gradually increasing the length of the cuts as you move up the face. By starting near the tip, you will remove the wood from the front of each successive cut, preventing uncontrolled splitting. Ensure that the face remains symmetrical by constant reference to the centre-line, re-drawing it if necessary to maintain it as a fixed point of reference. Gradually work back across the corners until the face has been rounded into the body.

To complete the rounding off, overlap the anti-clockwise cuts with clockwise cuts, again beginning at the tip of the nose. Make shallow cuts where the snout blends into the body, so that the centre of the hedgehog's back remains high (see Fig 6.11).

To finish off rounding the body and snout, cut outwards and over the sides of the remaining edges of the block, working up to the mid-way line, taking great care not to cut too deeply (see Fig 6.12). Continue until all surfaces fall away from the centre- and mid-way lines and the hedgehog is completely rounded, except for the base, which should remain flat.

Fig 6.12 Cut outwards and over the sides of the remaining edges of the block.

Final shaping and smoothing

The ridges left by the no. 9 gouge can be removed with the Surform or your largest no. 3 gouge, such as a 1in (25mm) ¾in (18mm) or ½in (13mm) V tool, and a mallet, cutting with the gouge bevel-down on the wood. Once the ridges have been removed, turn the gouge bevel uppermost and, still using the mallet, carefully slice towards the centre-line, guiding the tool around the shape with very shallow cuts (as shown in Fig 6.13). This will ensure that the corners of the blade do not dig in and score the surface. If this does happen, carefully pare away the scratch and the area surrounding it. Re-draw the centre- and mid-way lines each time they are removed.

Fig 6.13 Shaping with the wide no. 3 gouge held bevel uppermost.

If you have used a Surform, it will have left little ridges all over the piece (as shown in Fig 6.14). These can be removed with the large no. 3 gouge, bevel downwards, applying hand pressure only. Alternatively, use a convex-soled spokeshave.

Taking the centre-line as a reference, examine the shape of the wood on each side, running your hands over it to feel for any

Fig 6.14 The surface after smoothing with a Surform.

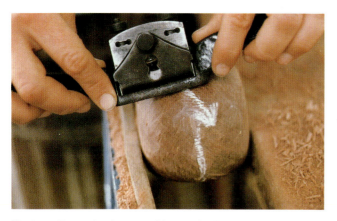

Fig 6.15 Removing bumps with a spokeshave.

Fig 6.16 Scraping the surface prior to detailing.

bumps or flat areas that remain. Mark these with chalk and remove them with shallow paring cuts, using the no. 3 gouge or spokeshave (see Fig 6.15). Run your hands over the carving again, and repeat the process until you are satisfied that the hedgehog is rounded smoothly. Remember that all the convex surfaces must flow away from the highest point, or the part that projects furthest.

Mark a line around the body, at right-angles to the centre-line, to show where the face meets the body. Then continue refining the shape of the face, using the same tools, making sure that it is symmetrical. Shave away a little more wood near the tip to leave it slightly longer than its final length. Leave the end flat, however, so that the hedgehog can still be held lengthways in the vice if necessary.

To leave a good clean surface for adding detail and texture, use a scraper to remove any remaining irregularities in the shape, or marks left by the spokeshave (as shown in Fig 6.16). Begin by working all around the nose, scraping outwards and towards the tip, and moving back along the body until you reach the mid-way line. Now turn to the

rear end and work in the same way, scraping towards the centre mark. When you reach the mid-way line, take particular care, as the grain will change direction where you meet the previously scraped wood. If the surface becomes woolly or dull looking, you have scraped beyond the mid-way line and will need to re-scrape this area in the opposite direction. Re-draw the mid-way line if necessary, to remind you.

Run your hands over the wood frequently to make sure you do not miss scraping any part of it. Do not forget the base, either.

Detailing the face

Draw on the eyes, nose and mouth, making sure that they are placed symmetrically. The nose will be left to last, as it is the most vulnerable detail. Using a ⅛ (3mm) or ³⁄₁₆in (4mm) 60° V tool, practise cutting around eyes on the end grain of a piece of scrap wood, of the same type as you are using, so that the effect is similar to carving the eyes on the hedgehog. Begin with a large circle, so that you can see what you are doing. Then, when you can make a good clean, completely circular cut that joins neatly at the same depth, graduate to one of the same size and shape as the hedgehog eyes. Try to complete each circle in one continuous sweep, moving your body accordingly as you cut.

When you are confident, move to your hedgehog, beginning the cut at the 3 o'clock position of the eye and cutting without stopping (see Fig 6.17). If you slip or make a mistake, do not panic. Simply pare back the surface with the ¼in (6mm) no. 3 gouge (doing the same to the other eye so that it matches), scrape, and try again.

Pare away the outer edge of the V cut, working outwards and with the grain towards the nose (see Fig 6.18), so that the eye stands proud of the surface. Use the corner of your ¼in (6mm) no. 3 gouge blade to do this, applying hand pressure to make a

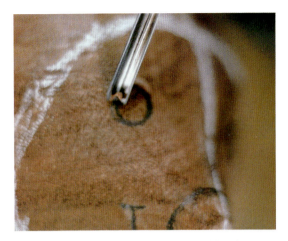

Fig 6.17 Cutting around the eye with a V tool.

slicing cut. Take care not to catch the corner of the blade in the eye as you work.

Then use the gouge as a scraper to remove any pencil marks from the surface of the eye, together with any gouge marks around it. Scrape with the grain, towards

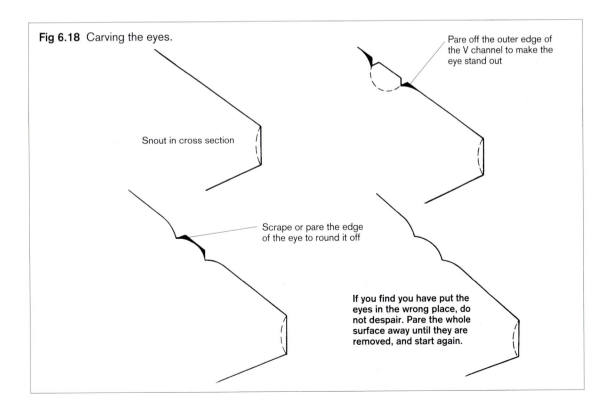

Fig 6.18 Carving the eyes.

Pare off the outer edge of the V channel to make the eye stand out

Snout in cross section

Scrape or pare the edge of the eye to round it off

If you find you have put the eyes in the wrong place, do not despair. Pare the whole surface away until they are removed, and start again.

Fig 6.19 Scraping around the eye using the ¼in (6mm) no.3 gouge as a scraper.

the tip of the nose (see Fig 6.19).

Carve the other eye in the same manner, matching its size and shape to the first.

Carving the mouth

Using the V tool, make a continuous cut from one end of the mouth to the other. Then round off the sharp edges of the cut with the corner of the ¼in (3mm) no. 3 gouge blade. Pare from one end of the mouth to the centre-line, and repeat from the other end to meet under the nose. Finally, scrape the pared surfaces gently with the edge of the gouge blade.

Adding the prickles

Draw the general lines of the prickles, starting with a fringe around the face and continuing along the body to converge at the centre-point of the rear end. The prickles will be represented by a series of short, even cuts made with a ¼in (6mm) 60° V tool. They must not run into each other and should be staggered row by row,

flowing tidily along the body.

Begin at the face end, about ⅜in (9mm) back from the fringe line and on the centre-line. Make a series of cuts towards the fringe line, so that each finishes on the line, working first around one side of the face, then the other. Use the mallet to drive the V tool, tapping it about five times before dropping your tool hand to lift out the chip cleanly. It may help to practise on some scrap wood first.

Place a second row of cuts behind the first, staggering them so that they do not run together. Continue in this way, row by row (see Fig 6.20), until the chips no longer come out cleanly. At this point, you will be quite close to the mid-way line and cutting along the grain. Remove each chip by nipping it off with the point of a ¼in (6mm) skew chisel, or the corner of your ¼in (6mm) gouge. When you find it impossible to cut any further without splitting the wood, stop, turn the carving around and begin texturing the rear end (as shown in Fig 6.21).

Begin at the centre-point of the rear end, making short cuts that converge on the

Fig 6.20 Texturing the front portion of the body.

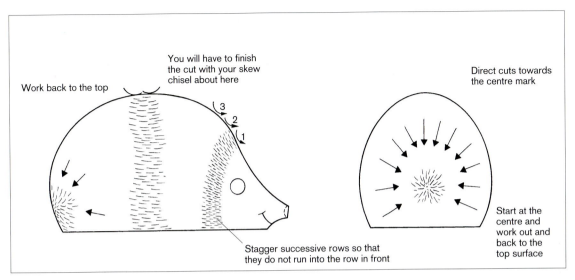

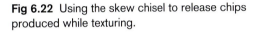

Fig 6.21 Texturing method.

centre-point. Work back towards the mid-way line, moving around the centre-point and gradually covering the rear end with cuts. Again, when the chips no longer come out cleanly, use the skew chisel or gouge to release them (as shown in Fig 6.22). Continue until you meet the cuts made on the front half of the hedgehog and the whole surface has been covered.

The short cuts will disguise any cracks or shakes that may have appeared as you worked.

Carving the feet

Draw the pads and claws on the base of the hedgehog. Cut the outline of each pad first, using the ¼in (6mm) 60° V tool, and working in one continuous sweep if possible. Then outline each claw with two V-cuts that meet in a point.

Carefully pare away the outer edges of the cuts, using the ¼in (6mm) no. 3 gouge, so that the pads and claws stand proud (as shown in Fig 6.23). Then scrape the pared surface smooth so that it blends into the base.

Fig 6.22 Using the skew chisel to release chips produced while texturing.

Fig 6.23 Paring around the feet.

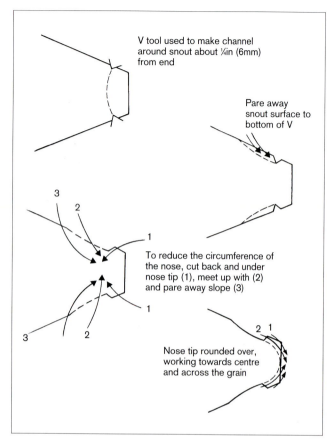

V tool used to make channel around snout about ¼in (6mm) from end

Pare away snout surface to bottom of V

To reduce the circumference of the nose, cut back and under nose tip (1), meet up with (2) and pare away slope (3)

Nose tip rounded over, working towards centre and across the grain

Fig 6.24 Carving the nose.

Fig 6.25 Reducing the size of the nose.

Fig 6.26 Rounding the nose.

Carving the nose

Draw a ring around the flat end of the snout and cut along it with the V tool in one sweep. This forms a channel into which the nose can be shaped to make it button-like. (see Fig 6.24). Very carefully shave away the snout surface where it meets the V-cut, using the ¼in (6mm) no. 3 gouge. Control these cuts so that you do not overshoot into the nose. At the end of each cut, do not lever the gouge, as you may remove the nose itself! If you withdraw the tool in the same plane as when cutting, the nose will be quite safe.

If the tip of the nose is too large, it can be reduced by cutting back and under from the nose side. Turn the gouge bevel uppermost, to match the curve of the nose tip, and make a cut around the shape (see Fig 6.25). This should be made at a steep angle so that you are cutting across the grain, and not directly into it, otherwise the wood will split. Continue cutting in this way all around the nose, then follow with more cuts from the snout side, making sure the cuts meet cleanly. Repeat the cuts until you have reduced the circumference of the tip to the appropriate size. Then pare away the snout side to blend it in with the rest of the face. Scrape the pared surface smooth with the end of the gouge.

To finish off the end of the nose, carefully round the outer edge by paring with the ¼in

(6mm) no. 3 gouge, held bevel uppermost. Work outwards and towards the centre of the tip, making slicing cuts (see Fig 6.26). Continue until the nose is perfectly round. Scrape it smooth, working towards the centre of the button.

Finishing

Examine the entire carving to make sure that there are no rough or sharp edges, or tiny whiskers of wood, that may catch in the polishing duster, paying particular attention to the texturing. Clean these up with the point of the skew chisel: its cutting edge can be used to scrape closely into the areas where the snout and nose tip meet, and around the eyes, mouth and feet.

Next, rub down the entire carving with 120 or 240 grit garnet paper, taking care not to make any carefully carved features indistinct. When working around these, fold the paper so that you can use a narrow edge to clean along the angle between two adjacent surfaces. Be prepared to spend a lot of time on finishing: if not carried out meticulously, your carving will lack quality.

Apply a coat of cheap, colourless wax polish to the surface, working it in with an old toothbrush. This will show up any remaining blemishes. These must be pared away, and the surrounding surface scraped and re-textured as necessary. When you are happy with the result, apply another coat of wax.

While the carving is still damp with the wax, rub it over with 240 or 320 grit garnet paper. The abraded dust will mix with the wax to leave a very smooth surface. Use the toothbrush to brush the excess wax from the prickle furrows, and run your hands over the carving to feel for any further imperfections. If you find any, these must be pared, scraped and finished as before.

Finally, coat the entire carving with a good quality, colourless wax. Leave it overnight, then buff it to a shine with a lint-free duster. Repeat this process several times to develop a patina, and handle the carving regularly, as this will also help build up a patina.

You have now completed your hedgehog, and if it is your first carving, you should be very proud of it. Show it off as much as possible and display it somewhere prominent. You have tackled a carving in the round, some relief and detail carving, texturing and finishing. Armed with these new skills, you should have the confidence and inspiration to begin another project.

Chapter 7

Introduction to Relief Carving

Heron

Relief carving offers you the opportunity of acquiring a wealth of skills that can be applied to many other carving projects, such as adding more detailed decoration to carvings in the round (like the hedgehog described in Chapter 6). Relief carving can also be used to decorate functional objects, such as turned bowls or dishes and items of furniture. With careful thought, this skill also makes it possible to personalize carvings given as gifts with a suitable motif or design. This heron is an ideal introduction to the technique.

Tools you will need

- ¼in (6mm) 60° V tool
- ⅛in (3mm) 60° V tool (optional)
- ½in (13mm) no. 3 (Swiss no. 2) gouge
- ¼in (6mm) no. 3 (Swiss no. 2) gouge
- ⅛in (3mm) no. 3 (Swiss no. 2) gouge
- ¼in (6mm) skew chisel

Choosing and preparing the wood

A piece of wood about 1in (25mm) thick is ideal for this type of work. It should be as straight-grained as possible, without any flaws or too strong a grain pattern, as this would distract the eye from the subject. Examine any strong patterning carefully to determine if you can incorporate it into your design, either as part of the background, or within the subject itself. I used a piece of lime for this project, but sycamore or any of the fruit woods, such as cherry or walnut, would be equally suitable. The piece of lime was approximately 14 x 10in (356 x 254mm). In this case, the grain of the wood runs horizontally to the image, but grain running vertically would also be acceptable.

Straighten all four edges of the wood by marking them with a square and planing them, remembering to work from the corners to the centre when planing along the grain and from the centre towards each corner when planing the end grain, to prevent the corners from breaking away. This done, smooth any sharp edges with abrasive paper, but do not sand the face to be carved, as any remaining dust from the sanding will blunt your tools.

Design

Always use a bold outline for a relief carving, and avoid too many small projections or fine detail. There are plenty of visual sources you can turn to for inspiration – books, magazines and pattern books, for example – and it is a simple matter to copy a design on to tracing paper with a pencil. You can even trace outlines from your own photographs of suitable subjects. Fix the paper in place with masking tape to prevent it from slipping. Hold the tracing over the wood and move it about until you are certain that no flaws in the wood will appear in key areas of the design (such as the middle of the head!). If you want to produce a reverse image of the original, simply turn the paper over before laying it on the wood.

Slip a sheet of carbon paper beneath the tracing paper and draw over the traced outline with a ballpoint pen, which ensures that you do not miss any of the pencil lines. Remove the tracing and carbon papers, and go over the outline on the wood with a pencil. Keep the tracing as your master copy, to record the different 'carving levels' (the order in which the relief will be carved) at a later stage.

Which way to cut?

The simplest and quickest way to begin is to carve around the outline using a 60° V tool, producing a V-shaped channel that subsequently can be deepened and widened with gouges. Do not forget that the V tool must always cut *with* or directly *along* the grain to obtain a clean edge to the outline, *never* against it. This way, any inadvertent tearing of the wood will be in the background to the relief, which will be carved away later.

Examine the direction of the grain in your wood (i.e. vertical or horizontal), and mark a line to represent this on your master tracing. Then systematically mark arrows around the outline only, showing the correct direction for carving with the V tool (see Figs 7.1 and 7.2). If you are in any doubt, imagine that you are working with the tool and it is about to slip. If this would cause the blade to dig into the outline of the relief, you are working in the wrong direction and should reverse your course. Once you have worked out the correct direction of carving on your master copy, transfer the arrows to the wood with a pencil.

Before you can begin work, it is essential that your piece of wood is held securely, using one of the methods described in Chapter 5. Whichever method you use, make sure you have plenty of room to walk around the work, and that you are able to unfasten and reposition it quickly, easily and securely.

Fig 7.1 Direction of V tool cuts with grain running across the figure.

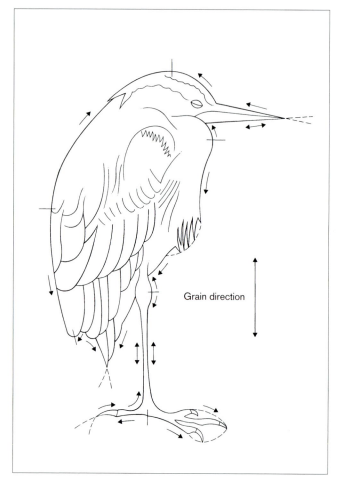

Fig 7.2 Direction of V tool cuts with grain running from top to bottom of the figure.

Outlining the design

The best tool for marking out your relief is a 60° straight-bladed V tool, as this gives the correct angle to guide subsequent cuts with other tools. A 45° tool would tend to make you undercut the outline, whereas a 90° tool might tear the surrounding wood unless you were extremely careful. A bent-bladed tool is almost impossible to guide accurately, while a deep U-shaped gouge will not produce the required sharp angle at the bottom of the groove.

Begin by practising on a piece of scrap wood, ideally of the same type as the actual workpiece. Use a mallet to control the tool and work in the manner described in Chapter 4. Do *not* hurry, but cut steadily, tapping gently with the mallet. Cut left- and right-hand curves, as well as channels that meet each other cleanly at the same depth, and lines that start at the same point and move away from each other. Finally, draw a few lines that correspond to portions of the outline of the heron, in the same grain direction, and cut these. By doing this, you will learn what the tool will do, how well you can control it and how the wood responds to it. When you are happy with the results, you are ready to begin cutting the outline of the heron (see Fig. 7.3).

Cut the V-channels in the same direction as the arrows marked on the wood. Always stop and begin again if you find that you are cutting into the design. Right-handers should always cut from right to left; left-handers from left to right. In this way, you will always be able to see where you are going.

The quickest method is to make all the cuts in one direction in one session, then all the cuts in another, and so on. This reduces the number of occasions when you will need to reposition the work or move around it, but whenever you find yourself needing to change direction to avoid cutting towards yourself, always adjust the work or move accordingly. In areas where the outline is a little intricate (such as around the feet), leave plenty of waste wood around the outline. These areas can be refined later, using small gouges.

Deepening the V-channels

You now need to deepen the V-channels and widen them, using the various sizes of no. 3 gouge.

First set of cuts

Prop the gouge in the channel, so that it rests against the heron (i.e. with the handle of the tool over the design and the direction of cut away from it), and at the same 60° angle as the wall of the cut (see Fig 7.4). Give the gouge a couple of taps with the mallet so that it cuts down the side of the channel and away from the outline, deepening that side of the groove. Slide the gouge along and repeat this action, working all around the outline. This cut will protect the design when you make the second set of cuts towards it.

Fig 7.3 Outlining the heron with the V tool.

Fig 7.4 Widening the V-channel: first cuts.

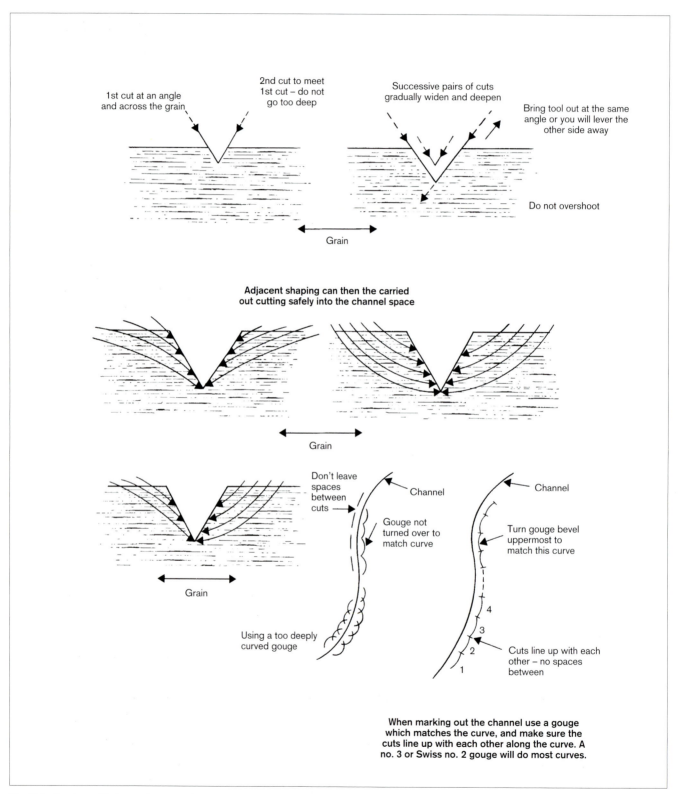

Fig 7.5 Cutting a V-channel across the grain.

Because the cutting edge of the gouge has a slightly curved cross-section, it must be turned so that its curve corresponds with that of the outline. This means that as you cut along the lines, sometimes you will be turning it one way, sometimes the other (see Fig 7.5). Use a wide gouge for shallow curves and a narrower gouge for the smaller, tighter curves and at sharp points, such as the end of the beak and claws. In these areas, overshoot with a little cross at the end to protect the tip (see Fig 7.6). If you notice the corners of the gouge digging into the outline, you are holding the tool the wrong way round, or using a gouge with an incompatible curve.

Second set of cuts

These are made *towards* the outline, also angled at 60°. They should meet the first set of cuts cleanly and at the same depth. This will have the effect of both deepening and widening the channel you made with the V tool (see Fig 7.7). Use the gouge with its bevel down for all of these cuts to obtain a cleanly-cut channel. If you make these cuts with the bevel uppermost by mistake, the corners of the blade will sink into the wood, producing a ragged chip that may remain attached to the body of the wood.

Start the cuts a little way from the outer edge of the channel, and aim them towards the outline. When you come to a curve, swing the tool around so that the whole of the cutting edge contacts the outline, not just a tiny part of it. As before, give the tool handle a couple of taps with the mallet, and if you have cut in at the correct angle, a clean chip should spring out. Holding the tool in

Fig 7.6 Widening the channel at the beak.

Fig 7.7 Widening the V-channels further.

the same manner, slightly overlap the edge of your previous cut and work around the outline to produce a deeper, wider channel than you made with the V tool.

If a chip does not come out cleanly, do not force it out by levering with the gouge, but leave it attached. This problem not only occurs when the tool is used bevel uppermost, but also if the initial set of cuts were made at too shallow an angle or not deep enough. As you will be repeating this cutting procedure several times, the chip will eventually be

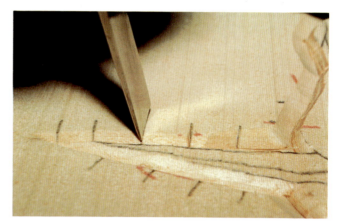

Fig 7.8 (left) Cutting the curve around the heron's head.

Fig 7.9 (below) Making 'firebreak' cuts along the beak.

released. Remember with all carving to keep the corners of the gouge blade free of the surface of the wood: do not let them sink in, as they will cause tears in the wood.

Cutting a channel along the grain

At the top of the heron's head, where the channel curves around and along the grain, you may find that the wood tends to split. You can prevent this by cutting in towards the outline, alternately from one side of the curve, then the other (see Fig 7.8), 'catching' the cut before it can 'run' and split the grain. Finish with a final cut in the centre.

Where you have to cut a long straight channel along the grain, after your initial cuts, place a series of 'firebreak' cuts along it at short intervals (see Fig 7.9). These will limit any splitting that might occur when you begin the second set of cuts towards the outline.

Having deepened the channel around the outline once, repeat the procedure, cutting downwards, deeper and away from the

design, then towards it from a little further away, until you have a clean channel about ¼in (6mm) deep and ¼in (6mm) wide. This channel will be used to work into as you clear away the background, leaving the heron raised in relief, ready for modelling.

Establishing the levels

Refer to your master copy of the heron again, and mark on it the background as level 1. This is the deepest area of wood to be removed, and it is carved away first. Level 2 is the next deepest and, in this case, is the underside of the bird. Level 3 is the leg, which is closer to you than the underside, in the same way that the base of the beak (level 4) is nearer to you than its tip. You will see from Fig 7.10 that various parts of the carving have corresponding levels of relief: the leg, beak and some of the feathers all at level 3; the tips of the claws, other areas of feather, the back of the head and the base of the beak all at level 4; and so on. Mark all the ascending levels on the master copy. These not only show the level of relief, but also the order in which each portion should be carved. The overall effect you want to achieve is a rounded shape with the highest area at the shoulder (level 7). There is no limit to the number of levels you have, but remember that each must blend imperceptibly into the next.

Removing level 1: the background

I made the required gentle slope down towards the heron using a ½in (13mm) no. 3 gouge, but a no. 4 or 5 could also be used if you wanted a more patterned effect. Before you begin, to save time and tedious tidying up later on, make sure that your tools are razor sharp. This will ensure that each cut you make is burnished and clean enough to be left as a final surface. As you work, if the freshly cut surfaces begin to appear dull or torn, stop and re-sharpen your tools. Then go back over these areas again.

Begin close to the edge of the V-channel and cut forwards into it, removing its edge down to the bottom of the channel, but without cutting into the outline of the heron. Start the second row a little further away from the edge you have removed, and overlap rows of cuts with more cuts so that you produce a gentle slope (see Fig 7.11). Drive the tool slowly as you approach the heron's outline, keeping the cuts shallow by using only the centre of the cutting edge, which will prevent the wood from splitting.

Fig 7.10 The various carving levels.

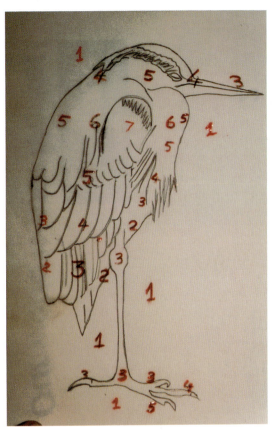

Fig 7.11 Carving away the background.

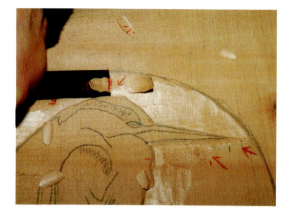

Fig 7.12 Cut in both directions to remove chips when cutting along the grain.

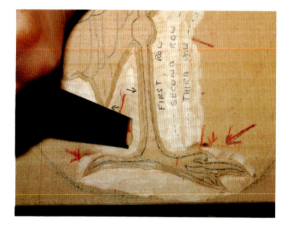

Fig 7.13 Divide the waste into two halves in confined areas.

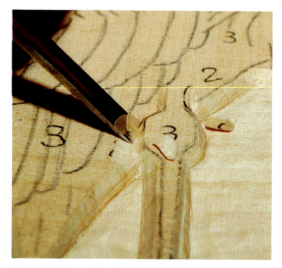

Fig 7.14 Deepening the channel around the leg.

Continue this process, cutting towards the bird all the time, until you reach the edge of the background area. Do not blow the chips away in case they fly into your eyes. Remove them with a brush, not your hand, to avoid the risk of splinters.

At the top of the head and beneath the feet, where you have to clear away along the grain, tilt the gouge and cut parallel to the grain in one direction, then detach the resulting chip by cutting towards it at the same depth and blade angle, but from the opposite direction (see Fig 7.12). Take care when cutting around any knots or flaws: you may need to reverse the direction to obtain a clean cut. In confined areas, divide the waste requiring clearing into two halves, and cut towards the nearer channel (see Fig 7.13).

Levels 2 and 3

These are the underside of the bird, the leg, the tip of the beak, the outer edge of the back and the areas that adjoin the background. You can use a very sharp V tool, or make opposing cuts, using a ¼in (6mm) or ⅛in (3mm) gouge, to cut a channel around the upper leg where it overlaps the underside of the bird. That is to say, around level 3, and over the sides of the outline, to link up with the leg. Deepen this channel if necessary, using the appropriate gouges (see Fig 7.14). Then shave away the surface of level 2 to leave the leg standing proud of its surroundings. As before, cut into the channel you created, then shave it with overlapping cuts to clear away the area. Now work over the edge of the bird's back with shallow cuts (see Fig 7.15). Keep the gouge bevel down to remove each chip, across the edge, at the same time lifting your gouge hand to cleanly curve the edge so that it meets the background tidily. Because the outline of the bird is rounded, repeat this process all around the edge. Be careful when rounding the leg: it has very short grain running across it and is delicate. Cut from the middle outwards to each side, which will prevent a piece from breaking out (see Fig 7.16).

When you round the top of the head, you will also need to take care to cut in the correct direction: outwards from the centre. Shave the beak tip so that it is tapered, working towards the tip on the upper part, and possibly towards the body of the heron on the lower mandible, depending on the grain of the wood and the position of your design. Then re-draw the feathers over the rounded edges and in the areas that have now been lowered.

Levels 3, 4 and 5

Cut channels along the edges of the feathers on level 4, using a V tool or appropriate no. 3 gouge. Make opposing cuts as before (see Fig 7.17), then shave away the surface (level 3), joining the ends

Fig 7.15 Work over the edge of the bird with shallow cuts.

Fig 7.16 Rounding the leg.

Fig 7.17 Cutting around the feathers.

Fig 7.18 Shave away the surface to make the feathers stand proud.

Fig 7.19 Remove the right-hand side of each feather channel.

Fig 7.20 Leave the other sides so that the feathers appear to overlap.

Fig 7.21 Cut a channel around the shoulder and up to the crop.

Fig 7.22 Remove levels 5 and 6 where the beak joins the crop.

of the cuts as you work outwards, and into, the channel (see Fig 7.18). The feathers will then stand proud.

Overlap the feathers by carefully shaving along the length of each feather, removing the right-hand side of each channel (see Fig 7.19) and leaving the other side as the adjoining feather edge (see Fig 7.20).

Levels 5, 6 and 7

Cut a channel around the shoulder and up to where the heron's beak joins the crop, using the V tool or a suitable no. 3 gouge (see Fig 7.21). Deepen this channel, as described previously, using the opposing-cut technique. Now cut in towards the shoulder to leave it raised. Next, shave away levels 5 and 6 over the back, where the beak joins the crop, and around the edges of the wing (see Fig 7.22).

Carefully shave away the head so that it is below the level of the shoulder, and re-draw the eye. Chamfer the edges of the beak (which has already been tapered), paring carefully to leave the highest level of relief along the middle of the beak. You may need to cut towards the crop on the lower

section, and towards the tip on the upper, at the same time working slightly across the grain (see Fig 7.23). Cut towards the tip with the V tool to mark the middle line, then around and over the crop to meet the beak and the lower part of the head.

The head now needs to be rounded away from its highest point, on the crown. Carefully shave away the surfaces on each side of the crown so that they fall away, and re-draw the eye. This can be carved in next, using a ⅛in (3mm) gouge (not the V tool, which would damage such a small detail). Cut a channel around the eye, being sure to cut away from the outline first, then carefully cut towards this channel (see Fig 7.24). Do not lever the chip, but pare away the adjacent surface to leave the eye standing proud. Then round off the ends (see Fig 7.25), turning the gouge bevel uppermost to curve the surface and cut a line for the eyelid (see Fig 7.26). Remove the lower corner, using the point of the skew chisel if the ⅛in (3mm) gouge is too wide.

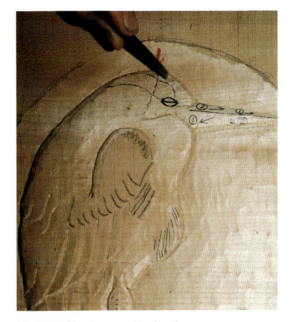

Fig 7.23 Shaving away the head.

Fig 7.24 Shaping the eye.

Fig 7.25 (below) Rounding the ends of the eye.

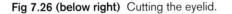

Fig 7.26 (below right) Cutting the eyelid.

Fig 7.27 Re-carving the ends of the feathers.

Fig 7.28 Texturing the fine feathers.

The remaining wing feathers can be carved as before, by cutting channels around each feather and making them overlap by removing the lower surface that adjoins each end. Carefully re-carve the edge of each feather, which will have been removed previously so that they again meet the ends of the feathers in the row above (see Fig 7.27). To mark the centre shafts of the primary feathers, gently cut a fine channel along the length of each feather, using a ¼in (6mm) no. 3 gouge or a very sharp V tool.

The toes need to be defined by cutting away the wood around them, and making a channel into which the edges of each toe can be pared and the ends of the claws pointed. Be careful not to delve too deeply between the toes. Use a skew chisel or ⅛in (3mm) no. 3 gouge to tidy up the ankle, where cuts from one direction meet those from the other. Once you have pointed the claws, use a ⅛in (3mm) gouge or a skew chisel to cut a channel across each toe to delineate them. This concludes the relief carving of the heron, which is ready to be textured.

Texturing

The small, fine feathers along the wing and on the breast, and the colour-contrasted area on the head, are carved using either the V tool or the ¼ or ⅛in (6 or 3mm) no. 3 gouges. Cut fine channels, in the same way as you carved the centre shafts of the primary feathers. Follow the drawn lines as far as possible, and bring the detailing right over the rounded edges to meet the adjacent surface – the background itself, in the case of the breast feathers (see Fig 7.28).

To texture the striped area around the eye and across the head, I used a small ⅛in (3mm) V tool, holding it as if it was a pen, and flicking out the chips to make little nicks in the surface.

Undercutting

Prop the carving up so that you can stand back and scrutinize it. Inevitably, you will see one or two places around the edge of the heron (especially on the sides of the legs) that would benefit from shadowing, to make the bird appear more rounded and give more depth. This effect is achieved by undercutting and hollowing beneath the edges. I also decided to adjust the shape of the back of the heron's neck, as I felt that the hollow behind the neck was not distinctive enough. I did this by paring down the edge of the outline, and cutting in a little more from the background.

To begin the undercutting, pencil along the edges you think would be improved by shadow, and stand back again to view the effect. This will give you a reasonable idea of how the undercutting will look before actually trying it.

Once you have decided upon the areas that will benefit from undercutting, select the widest gouge that will fit the shape of the outline and rest the bevel against the edge of the relief, so that the bevel is vertical. Cut down into the background, making the cut no deeper than any texturing on the background. Remove the chip by cutting towards it, in line with the surface of the background. Repeat the process, tilting the gouge a little more with each downward cut so that the gouge handle is over the background. The horizontal cuts will extend the background slightly beneath the edge of the relief (see Fig 7.29).

Do not get carried away: undercut only enough to produce a shadow. If you remove too much wood, the edges of the relief will become too fragile. For this reason, undercutting should always be left until last, apart from any necessary tidying up.

Tidying the work

Remove all your pencil lines with an eraser; don't use abrasive paper, as this will dull the burnished tool cuts you have worked so hard

Fig 7.29 Undercutting the leg.

to produce and remove the crisply carved edges. Check all around the outline where the heron meets the background, paring below any deep cuts and severing any fibres that remain where one surface meets another. Make sure that the rounded edge is cleanly cut, again paring away any unintentional grooves or humps. No. 3 (Swiss no. 2) gouges are the best tools for this type of tidying up. Remember to sharpen them first to ensure that all the cuts are clean and shiny. If necessary, gently extend the background area out to the edges of the board, so that the whole surface is lightly tooled.

Carefully clean up any poor cuts, such as at the end of the beak and claws where it is easy to dig the tool in too deeply. Then use a no. 3 gouge, with its bevel uppermost, as a scraper to remove any unwanted facets or ridges on the surfaces that should be smooth. Do not forget to work with the grain when you are doing this: if the surface becomes dull and woolly looking, you are scraping against the grain, so stop and reverse direction. You will find the skew chisel useful as a scraper in confined spaces, and also for slicing away any remaining fibres in tight corners and angles.

Finally, step back to view the carving from all sides. This will reveal any further blemishes that need cleaning up.

Finishing

I used Danish oil as the finish for this piece, as it brings out the colour and any patterns in the wood, which is ideal with the rather bland and uniform lime. You could use a clear wax polish instead, but it will take longer for the colour of the wood to be brought out.

Shake the can of oil well and apply the finish with an old toothbrush. Wipe off any excess oil and leave the carving overnight to allow the oil to soak in. Once dry, apply a good quality colourless wax polish (also with the toothbrush), then buff the surface to a shine with a lint-free duster. The project is complete!

Chapter 8

Simple Hollowing Techniques

Bowl

At an early stage in your carving career, you are likely to have to carve some hollows, and carving a bowl is a good introduction to the techniques. Once learned, these will allow you to cope with all shapes and sizes of hollow form, whether in the round or in relief. The bowl in this project is a tactile shape, made from a nicely patterned wood, with both concave and convex surfaces, the latter requiring the rounding techniques used to make the hedgehog in Chapter 6. Also shown are various methods of decorating and embellishing bowls or platters, including the technique of relief carving.

Choosing and preparing the wood

Most of the woods listed in the glossary on page 175 can be used for a bowl, but sycamore and beech are traditionally employed for bowls that will contain food. Both are close-grained and can be scrubbed clean. Avoid yew and laburnum,

Tools you will need

- ½in (13mm) no. 9 gouge
- 1in (25mm) no. 3 (Swiss no. 2) gouge
- ¼in (6mm) no. 3 (Swiss no. 2) gouge
- ½in (13mm) no. 5 gouge
- Surform
- Stick-bladed Surform or rounded riffler (optional)

- Convex-soled spokeshave
- Cabinet scraper
- Table knife scraper, ground with a rounded end (optional)
- Saw

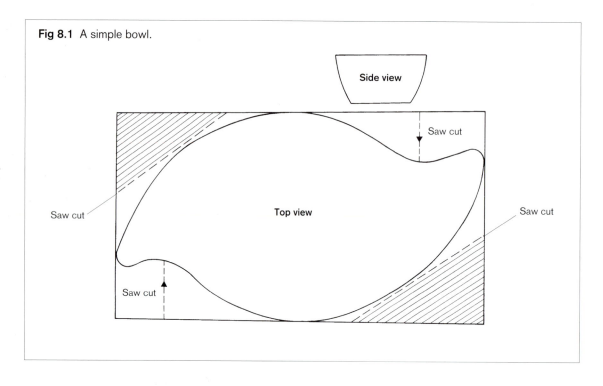

Fig 8.1 A simple bowl.

Side view

Saw cut

Top view

Saw cut

Saw cut

Saw cut

as they are toxic. Whatever wood you choose, the piece must be straight-grained and free from flaws, with the grain running along the length of the bowl. A close grain will be easier to finish smoothly, but may not have such an interesting pattern as a coarse grain. However tempting it may be, do not use a slice from a tree trunk, as it will be very difficult to work, being mostly end grain.

Freshly cut wood will be easier to work, but bear in mind that it could crack or distort as it dries. If you do not know how seasoned the piece is, keep it in a polythene bag or wrapped in Clingfilm when not working on it, placing any chips you have removed in the hollow. Alternatively, wrap it in a damp cloth to slow the drying process. Hollowing the bowl will relieve the stresses that cause cracking, and as you progress you will be

able to dispense with the protective wrapping.

I chose a plum log, about 6in (150mm) in diameter and 8in (200mm) long, which I split down the middle with an axe and hammer, intending to make matching bowl from the unused half in due course. Alternatively, you could use a turning blank, purchased ready cut from a good timber supplier, or a rectangular block of appropriate size.

Examine the grain pattern carefully and decide which will be the top and base of the bowl. Depending on the way in which the wood has been cut, the grain pattern may be symmetrical, providing an even marking around the inside of the bowl. If necessary, remove any bark and loose areas with a wide no. 3 gouge and mallet, or a Surform. Then plane the bottom of the wood so that it will stand without rocking, and, using the Surform, a plane or a no. 3 gouge, clean the upper surface so that it can be drawn on.

Rough-shaping the exterior

Draw the outline of the bowl on the top surface of the wood, making it as large as the wood will allow. You can do this either by copying it on to tracing paper and transferring the tracing to the wood with carbon paper, or by making a cardboard template and drawing around it (see Fig 8.1). Saw off each end of the wood at an angle to match the shape of the bowl (see Fig 8.2), and make a shallow saw cut to the bottom of each concave section. This will help in removing the wood from these areas.

Round over the sawn ends with the ½in (13mm) no. 9 gouge, which will remove the wood quickly. Then go over the surface again with the 1in (25mm) no. 3 gouge, followed by a Surform to remove the ridges. Work so that you are cutting out towards the ends of the wood, i.e. with the grain, at all times. For the time being, leave the central areas of the sides flat and parallel to each other, so that the bowl can be held easily in the vice.

Turn the bowl on one side and begin shaping the concavity using the 1in (25mm) no. 3 gouge with the mallet. Cut down from each side towards the saw cut that runs to the depth of the concave area (as shown in Fig 8.3). As you reach the bottom of the saw cut, make your gouge cuts longer and

Fig 8.2 Remove the marked waste wood at the corners by sawing.

Fig 8.3 Remove waste from concave areas by cutting towards the saw cut from each side.

shallower by dropping your tool hand to scoop out the chips, so forming a gentle hollow. Carefully extend this around the edge and into the rounded surface underneath. Then turn the wood over and repeat this process at the other end. With care, a stick-bladed Surform or rounded riffler can be used in the hollows to blend the surfaces together.

Now round over the sharp edges at the rim of the bowl, using the gouge with hand pressure only. Hold it with the bevel uppermost when working on the convex

Fig 8.4 Rounding over the edges of the rim.

Hollowing out

Before you hollow out the interior of the bowl, draw the inner edge of the rim on the top face, about ¼in (6mm) in from the edge. Then draw a line across the width of the bowl, at the deepest part (the centre), which will be the point at which you have to change direction as you cut, otherwise you will be working against the grain (see Fig 8.5).

Hollowing is begun by cutting a channel across the deepest part of the bowl, then widening and deepening it until you achieve the desired shape and depth. This is the correct method for making a hollow of any size or shape. You could have used this technique instead of making saw cuts when roughly shaping the exterior of the bowl, but sawing speeds the process.

Fix the bowl in the vice, with the top face

areas (see Fig 8.4), and bevel down in the concave areas. Watch carefully which way to cut, changing direction if a chip does not come away cleanly: it is easy to split the edge if you are not careful. Finally, work over the whole exterior surface with the Surform until the bowl feels pleasant in your hands. At this point, you are ready to begin hollowing.

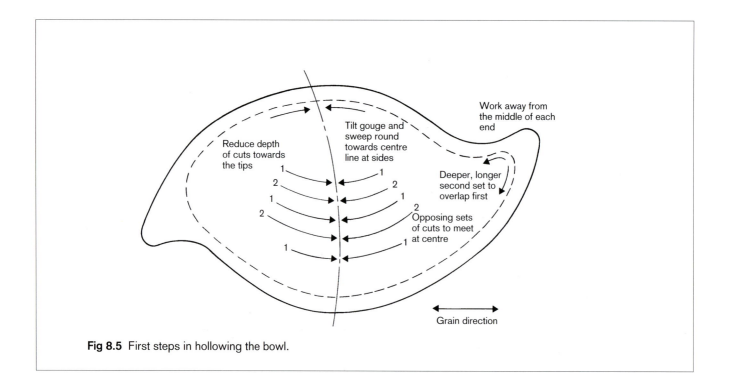

Fig 8.5 First steps in hollowing the bowl.

uppermost and the base resting on a block of wood so that it cannot drop as you work. If you experience difficulty in gripping the bowl securely, wrap it in a damp cloth first. Using the ½in (13mm) no. 9 gouge and mallet, begin cutting down towards the central pencil line, beginning about ½in (13mm) away from it (see Fig 8.6). Make shallow cuts so that the corners of the gouge are always above the surface of the wood, and leave the chips attached. Having worked from one side of the bowl to the other, turn it around (or move so that you will not be cutting towards yourself) and repeat the process along the other side of the line, making cuts of the same angle and depth to release the chips cleanly (see Fig 8.7). If you cut too deeply, some chips may remain attached, but do not lever them out with the gouge, as you may split the

wood. Simply leave them in place; they will be removed as you continue to widen and deepen the channel (see Fig 8.8).

Fig 8.6 Cutting the first groove across the area to be hollowed.

Fig 8.7 (right) Make a series of cuts towards the central line, then turn the bowl around and repeat the series of cuts to remove the chips.

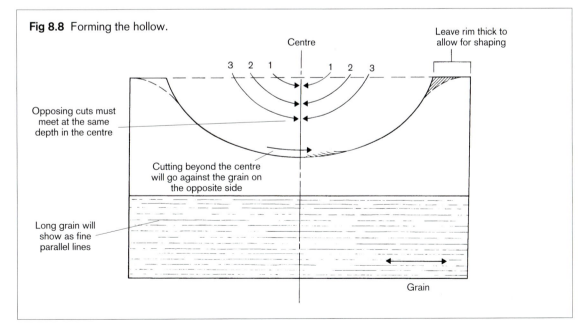

Fig 8.8 Forming the hollow.

Leave rim thick to allow for shaping

Centre

3 2 1   1 2 3

Opposing cuts must meet at the same depth in the centre

Cutting beyond the centre will go against the grain on the opposite side

Long grain will show as fine parallel lines

Grain

Fig 8.9 Round over the inner edge of the rim.

Fig 8.10 Work with a slicing action to obtain a smooth, rounded surface.

Turn the work around and overlap the first row of cuts with a second, deeper row, beginning a little further back. Then turn it again and repeat the process. Continue in this fashion, row by row, making sure that the opposing cuts on each side of the central line are equal in depth and distance from the line. Always cut towards the line. As the hollow becomes deeper, you can achieve a scooping action with the tool by dropping, then lifting, your gouge hand.

Having removed the bulk of the waste from the hollow, change to the flatter ½in (13mm) no. 5 gouge and use it to remove the ridges left by the no. 9 gouge. At the sides of the bowl, twist the tool so that it is tilted and cutting slightly across the grain, so that its corners cannot dig into the walls. As you approach the ends of the bowl, use longer strokes and gradually reduce the depth of the cuts to produce a gentle slope towards the centre. When you find your tool is obstructed by the edge and you can go no deeper, carefully form the hollow to the shape of the rim, rounding over the top edge (as shown in Fig 8.9).

Smoothing the interior

Having removed the ridges from the initial hollowing out, use the ½in (13mm) no. 5 gouge by hand as if it is a small plane, pushing it forwards with your tool hand, but restraining the blade at the same time with your other, so that it cuts shallow slices in a very controlled manner. On the curve where the walls meet the bottom of the hollow, twist the tool slightly so that the width of the blade is used with a slicing action to obtain a smooth, rounded and hollowed surface (as shown in Fig 8.10). This is a very useful technique to master, and one that is used frequently in carving.

At the centre line, a slicing cut slightly across the grain may help, especially with a coarser wood. Work systematically over the

104

entire surface, removing tiny fine shavings and keeping the tool bevel pressed firmly against the surface. Continue until the hollow is as smooth as you can make it, and the surfaces at the centre meet each other cleanly and at the same depth.

Run your fingertips over the surface, feeling for any irregularities. Mark any you find with pencil and shave them away. Then scrape the pared surface with the end of the ¼in (6mm) no. 3 gouge, taking care to prevent its corners from scoring the surface. If this happens, use a narrower no. 3 gouge. Begin scraping at the centre and work back towards each end, but remember to scrape with the grain towards the centre. An old table knife, with its blade cut to a length of about 1in (25mm) and ground to a rounded end, makes a very effective scraper for hollows (see Fig 8.11).

If you do not intend using your bowl for food, apply a coat of cheap colourless wax polish to reveal any flaws or remaining irregularities in the surface. Remove them by paring or scraping. If you wish to use the bowl for food, don't apply wax, but continue as before, until you have removed all the imperfections.

When you are satisfied with the surface, abrade the hollowed area with 320 grit garnet paper, wrapped around a piece of foam rubber, so that it achieves good contact with the surface as you rub. Do not blow the dust from the bowl in case it gets into your eyes: tip it out, or wipe it away using a damp cloth.

Fig 8.12 Shape the outer surface to correspond with the inner.

Completing the exterior

Place the bowl upside down in the vice, standing the rim on a flat block of wood that is longer than the bowl. Tighten the vice just sufficiently to prevent the bowl from slipping – a damp cloth will help prevent this.

With the ½in (13mm) no. 9 gouge and mallet, start at one end of the bowl and cut outwards to reduce the thickness of the walls to about ¼in (6mm), so that the outer surface corresponds with the inner (see Fig 8.12). Then go over the surface with a flatter gouge,

Fig 8.11 A table knife can be ground to make an effective scraper.

such as a ½in (13mm) no. 5 or no. 3. You will need to estimate the thickness of the walls by using your fingers like a pair of callipers, marking any lumps or hollows with a pencil, then removing them. Repeat the process for the other end of the bowl, until the outer surfaces match the inner, and the walls are uniform for the entire bowl.

When you are satisfied, place the bowl on its side in the vice, inserting a long flat piece of wood between the vice jaws and the rim to spread the pressure and prevent accidental cracking. Carefully shave the outer surface with the convex-soled spokeshave, working towards the ends from the centre, until the exterior is nicely rounded. Alternatively, a Surform used with a light forwards action, or a wide no. 3 gouge held bevel uppermost, could be used in place of the spokeshave. Make sure you cut in the correct direction at the centre of the bowl (i.e. with the grain), which will be most rounded. Then repeat the process for the other side until the entire bowl feels smooth and the same thickness between your fingers.

Finishing

Having obtained smooth walls of even thickness, go over the exterior of the bowl with the cabinet scraper, taking care to scrape down towards the bottom of the hollows, and away from the centre towards the ends. Lightly abrade the surface with 320 grit garnet paper, wrapped around a piece of foam rubber, until the bowl feels completely smooth in your hands.

If you wish, you can glue felt to the base at this stage. Cut the felt to shape and score the

wood with a knife or skew chisel to provide a good key for the glue. Then apply PVA adhesive to the centre of the base, press on the felt from the centre outwards, and cut the felt to final shape when the glue has dried.

If your bowl is to be used for food, you can burnish the surface by rubbing a handful of the wood chips firmly against it to develop a sheen. Other good finishes to bring out the colour would be liquid paraffin, which is tasteless and odourless, or an edible oil such as almond, olive or lemon. However, since I did not intend using my bowl for food, I applied Danish oil to seal the wood and bring out its colour. It was allowed to soak in overnight and followed by several coats of a good quality wax polish, buffed to a shine with a lint-free duster (see Fig 8.13).

Coping with flaws and mistakes

Cracks and splits may appear in your bowl if it has been made from unseasoned wood and allowed to dry out too quickly. If these are very fine, after completing the carving, treat the cracked area with a cheap colourless wax polish and rub the bowl down with 320 grit garnet paper. The abraded wood dust will mix with the wax and fill the hairline cracks. Wider cracks can be filled with PVA glue and sawdust or slivers of wood, as described in Chapter 1. After allowing the glue to set, the damaged areas can be re-finished in the normal manner.

In the unfortunate event of breaking through the wall of the bowl, other than inserting a patch, little can be done, unless you convert the bowl into a small dish. Prepare the hole for patching by cutting away its edges until you reach wood that is thick enough to support a patch about ⅛–¼in (3–6mm) thick. Place some paper behind the hole and copy the outline with a pencil. Transfer this to a matching piece of wood that is slightly thicker than the wall of the bowl, making sure that the grain runs in the correct direction. Cut out the patch with a coping saw and glue it into the hole, securing it with masking tape on each side. Leave the glue to dry overnight, then shave and scrape both inner and outer surfaces until they are flush and the patch blends in with the rest of the bowl, although it will always be visible.

If the rim becomes damaged, it will need paring down to below the level of the damage. Remember to pare into the hollow along the inner edges of the rim, and towards the exterior along the outer edges, otherwise you may lift out a piece in error. A fragile rim can be reinforced by rubbing PVA glue into it with your fingers before paring and scraping.

Adding relief carving, patterns and textures

There is considerable scope when it comes to carving decoration into a bowl or platter. The examples shown overleaf are merely suggestions to get you started; once you are proficient with your tools, you will be able to experiment further, gaining inspiration from a variety of sources.

It is essential not to become over

Fig 8.13 The finished bowl.

enthusiastic: a simple decoration or repetitive pattern is often more effective than an elaborate covering of intricate carving. Study the pattern in the grain of the wood, and decide whether any flaws, such as knots, can be used to advantage in your design. Sometimes a strongly patterned wood is better left plain, or just very lightly tooled, yet bland woods can be much enhanced.

Give some thought to how the finished bowl or platter will be used: will it be functional or purely decorative? Is it to be personalized in some way? Remember that if the piece is to be functional, carved projections or minute undercut edges will crumble, snag or break, while soft wood will be easily dented, and sharp edges can injure hands.

Relief carving

In the example shown, the techniques employed in carving the heron in Chapter 7 were used to decorate the inside of the bowl. Moreover, by placing the design carefully, it was possible to incorporate a flaw in the wood.

As in normal relief carving, you can use any wood that is straight-grained and sound, but avoid those that appear to be striped with interlocking grain, no matter how pretty they may appear, as the wood will be tiresome to work. I chose a ready cut bowl blank, which are available in a vast range of sizes and woods from good timber suppliers. They are intended for woodturners, but are equally suitable for bowl carvers. The blank was of cedar and measured about 3in (75mm) thick and 10in (254mm) in diameter, which I could hold easily in my largest vice. Cedar is quick and easy to work, becoming extremely aromatic after a while.

Shallow relief carving the inside of the bowl

In this case, the bowl should be hollowed before shaping the outside, allowing it to be held more securely in the vice while you are carving the relief. Do not go too deeply, however, otherwise you will restrict your access when marking out the design with the V tool. Smooth the hollow to allow you to draw on it, but do not use abrasives, as the residual dust will blunt your tools quickly. Scrape or plane the top of the rim, rounding over the outer edge so that it is not sharp, and you are ready to begin carving.

As in all relief carving, use a design that is bold and clear, without any intricate projections. I traced the outline of a flamingo from a book, transferring it to the wood so that the bird appeared to be pecking at a knot, and using the striped pattern in the wood to represent water. The outline was carefully cut around with a ¼in (6mm) 60° V tool (as shown in Fig 8.14), working with the grain to give a clean edge to the outline. Relief carving applied to an object that is to be functional must be very shallow, otherwise its edges will break. In this case, I left the incised V-groove as a simple, cleanly cut channel (see Fig 8.15).

Fig 8.15 The finished flamingo.

Fig 8.14 Outlining the flamingo design.

Fig 8.16 (left) This relief carving has been smoothed to contrast with the tooled background.

Fig 8.17 (below left) Contrasting surfaces were also used in this ivy-leaf design.

Fig 8.18 A deeper relief carving of ivy leaves.

Relief with contrasting surfaces

In this example, the subject of the relief was a woman reading a book. As before, the design was traced and transferred to the wood with carbon paper, being outlined with a V tool. The background was then very lightly tooled, using a ½in (13mm) no. 3 gouge. This was begun by cutting to the depth of the V-channel around the relief, then gradually working back up the sides of the bowl to the rim. At the centre of the hollow, where a change of cutting direction is necessary, you need to cut half of each dimple from one side and leave the chip attached. This is released by cutting towards it from the other direction, working to the same depth for a clean, smooth surface. Experiment with various gouge sweeps to observe the possible effects, but avoid leaving sharp edges that may catch your hands.

I rounded the edge of the outline with the corners of a ¼in (6mm) no. 3 gouge, then gently smoothed the relief with a scraper, using the edge of the gouge in the more confined areas. This was followed by lightly abrading the scraped surface with 320 grit garnet paper to remove the tool marks completely (see Fig 8.16). Fig 8.17 shows ivy leaves carved by the same method. Contrasting surfaces are a simple and effective means of decorating a bowl, but limit yourself to two or three for the best effect.

An example of a deeper relief carving inside a bowl is shown in Fig 8.18. In this

Fig 8.19 Cutting bold vertical grooves in the side of a bowl.

Fig 8.20 Marking a border beneath the rim with a V tool.

case, the design was drawn on to a turning blank of yew, which was partially hollowed to leave an area for the ivy leaves, then the outer surfaces were shaped and virtually finished as before. The leaves were carved by outlining with a V tool, deepening the outline with the opposing-cut method, and finally undercutting along the edges into the hollow of the bowl. With this technique, it is essential not to make the undercut edges too fine, otherwise they may break.

Patterning outer surfaces

A rather bland looking bowl can be made more interesting by cutting bold vertical grooves with a deep gouge, such as a no. 9 or no. 10 (as shown in Fig 8.19). This requires a very sharp tool: any nicks or flaws in its cutting edge will leave a scored and scratched surface with each cut, so sharpen it before you start. You must cut each furrow with strong, confident, steady strokes, since any wiggles or deviations will be obvious.

As a guide for cutting the furrows, draw pencil lines from rim to base, so that they are slightly less than the width of the blade apart. This spacing will need tapering towards the base of the bowl if the sides are not vertical. In this case, the furrows will be deeper at the wide end than at the narrow end. You can leave a plain border under the rim, as in the example shown, by marking it with a V tool first (see Fig 8.20). Alternatively, the furrows can be taken right to the edge of the bowl, but to prevent the rim from breaking away as you work, they will need cutting from the rim downwards and from the base upwards, to meet cleanly in the middle.

Practise cutting parallel grooves on scrap wood first, with both constant and tapering widths and depths, until you are confident that you have mastered the technique. Since there may be areas of your bowl where the furrows need cutting from opposing ends to meet in the middle, practise this technique, too.

Fig 8.21 (right) Diagonal grooves are very effective.

When working on the bowl, you may find areas where the gouge cuts one half of the furrow cleanly, but tears the other. This can be overcome by twisting the tool as it cuts forwards, so that half of the blade continues to cut cleanly, while the other half is lifted clear of the wood. When you reach the end of the furrow, turn the tool around and use the same technique to cut the opposite side of the furrow.

Diagonal grooves, made in the same manner, are also very attractive (see Fig 8.21), while the appearance of beaten pewter can be simulated by cutting deep dimples in the wood with a gouge such as a ½in (13mm) no. 5 (see Fig 8.22). For the latter effect, sharpen the tool before you begin so that each cut will be burnished and can be left as a finished surface. You can experiment with different widths and sweeps of gouge to produce a variety of patterns in this way.

The rope rim

A carved rope rim makes an attractive finish for a chunky bowl. In the example shown, I used a 10in (254mm) blank of cedar, which I hollowed using a 1in (25mm) no. 9 gouge, changing to a 1in (25mm) no. 7 as I cut deeper. The bowl was finished in the usual manner, leaving a fairly wide area for the rim.

To begin cutting the rope effect, draw a line around the circumference of the bowl, about ¼in (6mm) in from the outer edge of the rim. Use a ¼in (6mm) 60° V tool to cut a groove along this line, changing direction where necessary to ensure a clean cut. Shave

Fig 8.22 (middle) Dimpling is also attractive.

Fig 8.23 (bottom) Outlining the area of a rope rim with a V tool.

the surface up to the groove using a ½in (13mm) no. 3 gouge, so that the rim stands proud, then round over the edges and the outside of the rim with the same gouge, held bevel uppermost and used with slicing action.

Around the outside of the bowl, cut another V-groove (as shown in Fig 8.23), ¼in (6mm) below the rim and equal in width to

Fig 8.24 Round over the edges of the V-channels.

Fig 8.25 Having marked each rope strand, outline them with the V tool.

Fig 8.26 Cutting V-channels with a no. 3 gouge.

Fig 8.27 Smoothing each channel with cloth-backed abrasive.

the groove around the top. As before, round over the edge of the channel (see Fig 8.24), and remove a little of the surface below the groove, so that the rim resembles a sausage around the circumference.

Next, mark out the rope strands. Measure the circumference of the bowl with a flexible tape measure, and mark divisions approximately 1in (25mm) long, taking each pencil line right over the rounded surface. Within each division, mark the halfway point. Now draw the line of each strand from the point where one division line meets the inner groove, through the halfway mark at the very edge of the rim, to the point where the next division line meets the outer groove.

Cut along each strand line with the V tool (as shown in Fig 8.25). In some areas, such as in the end grain, you may need to change the direction of the cut at the halfway point and begin again from beneath the rim, making sure that the grooves meet cleanly. Be sure to stop if you see any signs of the surface tearing, and cut from the opposite direction. If you cannot obtain a clean cut with the V tool, resort to making a channel with opposing cuts from a ½in (13mm) no. 3 gouge. To do this, place the corner of the blade at the start of the strand and cut in (see Fig 8.26), at the same time rolling the width of its cutting edge from one end of the strand to the other. Repeat this action from the opposite side to create a cleanly cut V-channel.

Round over the edges of the grooves that indicate the strands, and remove any remaining sharp edges. Either scrape each groove smooth – a tedious task – or do as I did and use a narrow strip of cloth-backed abrasive, folded to fit and pulled around the groove to soften the surface (as shown in Fig 8.27). Finally, return to the inside of the bowl, sloping it smoothly to meet the inside edge of the rope rim (see Fig 8.28).

Straw and basketwork

Straw work looks very impressive, but it is quick and simple to carve, provided you keep your wits about you. For the example shown, I used a small turned bowl, of unknown species, that had been left in my workshop.

The first task is to lay out a grid of squares to match the width of your chosen no. 3 gouge. The job will take much longer if you pick a size that does not match a gouge width, but if you intend working around the entire bowl, you will have to adjust the size to obtain a number of whole squares. Cut along the horizontal and vertical lines with a ¼in (6mm) 60° V tool.

The edges of alternate squares must be lowered to give the impression of a woven finish, so mark these along the first row, then one square along on the rows above and below, so that they alternate horizontally and vertically (see Fig 8.29). Working down a row at a time, make a light cut downwards towards the groove, keeping clear of the neighbouring square. Then cut in towards the shaded chip. The quickest way to do the job is to make all the cuts in one direction at a time. Shave the surface away from each side of the square being worked on until the middle is slightly rounded, then repeat the process for the next row, being sure to begin one square higher or lower than in the previous row (see Fig 8.30).

Fig 8.28 Slope the insides of the bowl to meet the rope rim.

Fig 8.29 In straw work, the edges of alternate squares must be lowered to give the appearance of a woven finish.

Fig 8.30 Shave the sides of the squares until they are slightly rounded.

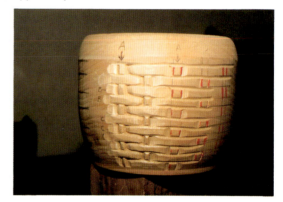

Fig 8.31 (left) Outlining a basketwork design with a V tool.

Fig 8.32 (below) Taper the ends of the runners on each side of a stave so that they are lower and appear to pass under it.

Next, scrape the surface smooth with the end of the no. 3 gouge, or a skew chisel.

You can vary this pattern by cutting tiny triangles from the corners of each tapered square, using the corner of your gouge blade.

Basketwork is a little more complicated, but is based on the same 'woven' principle. The upright portions of the design are called staves; the horizontals, runners. Marking out must be done correctly, as it is easy to make a mistake.

Draw on the vertical staves, shown as **A** in Fig 8.31, then the horizontal runners (**B**). Now mark the areas of the stave that will appear in front of the runners (**C**). These will alternate row by row, vertically and horizontally, as in straw work. To avoid confusion, erase the portions of the staves that will be behind the runners (**D**).

Cut along the horizontal lines first with a V tool, then use a ¼in (6mm) no. 3 gouge to cut vertically against the edge of each stave, where the runner passes behind it (**C**). As in straw work, taper the ends of the runner on each side of the stave, so that they are lower than the stave. Repeat this down the line (as shown in Fig 8.32). Then round over the edges of the runners and staves, and finish by scraping each smooth.

Chapter 9

Advanced Hollowing Techniques
Shell

Hollows of many shapes occur in most types of carving, and especially three-dimensional work. By making the bowl in Chapter 8, you learned simple hollowing skills; now you can progress to more advanced hollowing techniques within a spiral shape by carving this shell. In addition, the shell's tapered form requires the skills learned in Chapter 6 when making the hedgehog's snout.

Choosing and preparing the wood

Ideally for this carving, you need a log, which must be straight-grained, sound and knot-free. Since the carving will be hollowed out, you can use a section of a branch that is not completely seasoned, as the hollowing process will relieve the stresses that occur during drying and which cause cracking. In addition, the wood will be easier and quicker to work. You can use a square-sided block, but make sure that the grain runs lengthwise. You will have to convert it into a cylindrical shape before you begin work, by carefully splitting along the grain at each corner, using your widest no. 3 gouge with a mallet, and then smoothing the wood with the Surform or spokeshave. This is why it is easier to use a log if you can.

Tools you will need

- ½in (13mm) no. 9 gouge
- ½in (13mm) no. 3 (Swiss no. 2) gouge
- ¼in (6mm) no. 3 (Swiss no. 2) gouge
- ⅜in (9mm) no. 5 gouge
- ¼in (6mm) skew chisel
- Surform or convex-soled spokeshave
- Cabinet scraper
- Table knife scraper, ground with a rounded end (optional)
- 1in (25mm) no. 3 (Swiss no. 2) gouge (optional)
- ¼in (6mm) no. 9 or 10 gouge (optional)
- Saw

I chose a length of walnut branch from my store, but woods such as yew, plum, laburnum and acacia, which have contrasting colours of heart- and sapwood, would all be effective, because the deeper colour of the heartwood will show at the tip of the shell and in the hollowed area. The branch was about 3in (75mm) in diameter, and I cut it down to a length of about 5in (125mm), making sure that the ends were parallel so that it could be held easily lengthways in the vice. A longer piece of wood will produce more spirals; a greater diameter produces a more bulbous shell. It is not necessary to remove the bark before starting.

Fig 9.1 Remove a long, wedge shape from the log, just above and to the right of the aperture position.

Basic shaping

The apex of a shell is generally to the left of its aperture as you look at it (i.e. it spirals from left to right), so decide approximately where you want the aperture to be, mark it, then mark the position of the apex on the other end of the log. Sawing outwards and towards the apex, remove a long wedge-like section of the log from above the aperture position, and slightly to its right. This will produce the longest slope of the shell (see Fig 9.1), and is shown as section 1 in Fig 9.2.

Turn the wood a little to the right, and cut off section 2, a shorter wedge (marked 2 in Fig 9.3), followed in the same way by section 3 and section 4 (as shown in Fig 9.4). Removing these sections begins to create the basic lop-sided conical shape of the shell. Leave a flat area, about ¼in (6mm) square, at the tip, allowing the wood to be held easily lengthways in the vice.

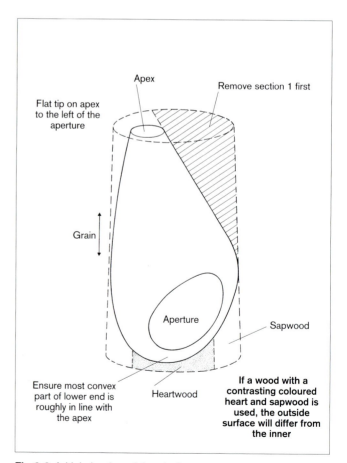

Fig 9.2 Initial shaping of the shell.

Fig 9.3 (above) Remove a shorter wedge from position 2.

Fig 9.4 (top right) Remove two more wedges, 3 and 4, to produce a lop-sided conical shape.

Rounding the base

Use a ½in (13mm) no. 9 gouge to round over the sharp edges at the base of the log, remembering to lift your gouge hand as you approach the sawn face, as described in Chapter 6 for shaping the rear end of the hedgehog. In the finished shell, the most convex part of the base should be opposite the tip, so with each stroke, guide the tool towards this point. Work all over the surface with short cuts, but make them gradually longer on the aperture side, rounding the wood right up to the aperture position (see Fig 9.5).

Shaping the apex

Remove the ridges between the adjacent sawn faces of the log, using the ½in (13mm) no. 9 gouge, working towards the tip. Cut with short strokes near the tip (sections 3 and 4), then lengthen them until the four faces have been blended together into a conical shape that leans to the left of the aperture position. Next, make a series of curving cuts around

Fig 9.5 (middle) Round the bottom of the shell.

Fig 9.6 (bottom) Make curving cuts around the upper portion of the shell.

the upper portion of the shell, beginning close to the apex and directing the cuts towards it (as shown in Fig 9.6). Extend the cuts so that they overlap around the end, as you did when shaping the hedgehog's snout in Chapter 6.

Fig 9.7 Smooth the entire piece of wood, then re-draw the aperture and spiral channel.

Fig 9.8 Widen the channel across the aperture with opposing gouge cuts.

Continue making the spiral cuts, carefully extending them along the aperture side until they meet up with the rounded base of the shell. Take care at this point, making shallow cuts and changing the direction of cut as necessary to work with the grain. You should aim to produce a continuous curved surface from the base to the apex.

Now work over the entire surface of the shell with the Surform, spokeshave or 1in (25mm) no. 3 gouge to smooth it, removing any remaining areas of bark at the same time. When working on the top half, cut towards the apex; on the lower half, work towards the most convex part of the base. If the shell tends to slip in the vice, turn it so that it is held lengthways, and cut towards the bench. Adjust the shape until it feels comfortable in your hands, making sure that there are no flat areas or depressions in the surface. If there are, remove them carefully by reducing the immediately adjacent areas. At this stage, the shell should resemble a lop-sided teardrop. Re-draw the outline of the aperture, and mark the position of the beginning of the spiral channel (see Fig 9.7).

Beginning the aperture

Using a ⅜in (9mm) no. 5 or ½in (13mm) no. 3 gouge, flatten the area within the aperture outline, then cut a slightly curved channel across the centre of the flattened area, beginning at the apex side. Hold the gouge with its blade almost vertical so that it cuts down and across the wood fibres. Do not lever the tool at the end of the cut, but leave the chips attached. After completing the first row of cuts, make a second row of opposing cuts, in the same manner, to remove the chips. If any chips do not come out cleanly, leave them, as further hollowing will eventually remove them.

Widen the channel with two more rows of opposing cuts, making them a little deeper and overlapping them (see Fig 9.8). Then deepen the centre, which will make it

Fig 9.9 (left) Scooping waste from the hollow.

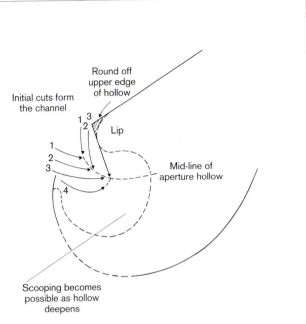

easier to remove wood with a scooping action of your hand. Round over the edge of the aperture so that the hollow can be enlarged further. When it is about ½in (13mm) deep, turn the gouge so that its bevel is against the edge of the aperture and gradually begin to cut back under the edge to form a lip, scooping back at a greater angle (as shown in Figs 9.9, 9.10 and 9.11). Continue to hollow out the aperture, working towards the lip and forming the shape towards the right in preparation for beginning the spiral channel.

Cutting the spiral channel

Draw the line of the spiral channel from the aperture around the shell and up to the right for a distance of about 1in (25mm). Using the ¼ or ½in (6 or 13mm) no. 3 gouge (not a V tool, as it will tear the grain), cut into this line from the apex side, then from the other

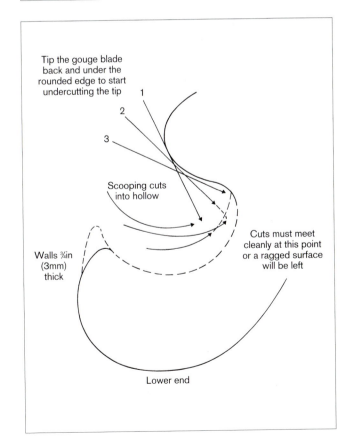

Fig 9.10 (top right) Deepening the aperture channel.

Fig 9.11 (right) Forming the aperture lip.

side to create a V-channel. When making these cuts, hold the gouge blade almost vertical so that it cuts deeply across the grain (as shown in Fig 9.12). Then pare away the lower edge and gradually working it back into the aperture to produce a gentle slope from the hollow, around the shell and up to the end of the channel. Now deepen the central area of the aperture a little more, undercutting the lip further and rounding it over. Adjust the shape of the aperture edge so that it flows smoothly into the channel (see Fig 9.13).

Next, begin to cut away from deepest area of the aperture to both left and right, scooping out the wood with the ⅜in (9mm) no. 5 gouge and cutting slightly across the

grain, as you did when hollowing the bowl in Chapter 8. You can do this by hand or with a mallet. Continue in this way until the inner surface corresponds to the shape of the outer surface, but leave the walls about ³⁄₁₆in (4mm) thick at this stage, so that the shell will withstand the pressure of the vice. Make the inner surface as smooth as possible as you hollow it out.

Return to cutting the spiral channel, extending it up and to the right for another 1in (25mm). As before, draw the line of the channel on the wood to ensure that it flows continuously around the shell. Make opposing cuts with the no. 3 gouge, making the channel about ¼in (6mm) deep and wide, and then rounding over both edges.

Next, remove the surface to the left of and above the channel. To retain the taper of the shell, this area will always need removing before cutting the next short section of

Fig 9.12 (top) Beginning the spiral channel.

Fig 9.13 (below) Adjusting the shape of the aperture edge and channel.

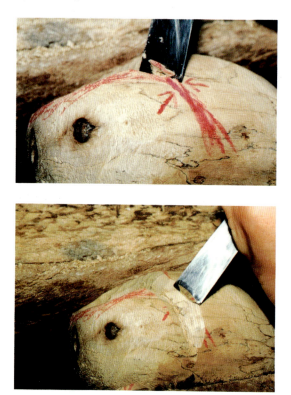

Fig 9.14 Continue cutting the spiral channel until you almost reach the top of the shell.

channel. Cutting a short section of the channel at a time, allows the curve of the spiral to be altered, which will be necessary since the shape and amount of taper of the shell will change as you progress.

Continue cutting the spiral channel in this manner, rounding its edges and removing the surface above and to the left until you almost reach the tip of the shell. As you progress up the shell, bring the spirals closer together. Leave the small flat area at the very tip, so that you can still hold the shell lengthways in the vice if required (see Fig 9.14).

If you want a more bulbous style of shell, cut the spiral channel deeper, as this will provide more depth to round into. Near the tip, watch for the change of cutting direction, which will be necessary on the top of each convex portion.

Smooth the complete shell with the no. 3 gouge, adjusting its shape, especially around the hollowed lower end, until it feels comfortable in your hands. Hold the gouge

Fig 9.15 Deepening the hollow.

bevel uppermost and use the corner of the blade to round over the sides of the spiral channel, so that it flows smoothly to the apex. Then scrape the entire outside of the shell with the cabinet scraper. You can use the point of a skew chisel or the ¼in (6mm) no. 3 gouge as a scraper to deal with the spiral channel, remembering to scrape in the correct direction along each side of the channel.

Completing the aperture

Make sure that the shell is held securely in the vice so that it cannot slip, as you will need to apply considerable pressure to it. Using the ½in (13mm) no. 9 or ⅜in (9mm) no. 5 gouge by hand, scoop the hollow deeper by levering the blade against the edge of the aperture, as shown in Fig 9.15. Note the positions of the hands, both of which should be used with the gouge and kept behind its cutting edge at all times – do not hold the carving in one hand and try to scoop with the other.

Slide the cutting edge sideways across the hollow, reducing the thickness of the walls and ensuring that the inner surface corresponds with the outer. As when carving the bowl in Chapter 8, gauge the thickness of the shell wall between your fingers and thumb, removing any bumps or hollows until it feels uniform.

Beneath the lip of the aperture, turn the gouge bevel uppermost and scoop downwards towards the deepest part of the hollow to undercut it further. Do not press too heavily upon the walls at the lower end, where you will be working in the end grain, as it could break out if mistreated. If this happens, alter the shape of the edge of the aperture and work more carefully. To provide better access for hollowing and further deepening of the aperture, enlarge it by cutting back the edge where the lip flows into the spiral channel.

As with other forms of carving, do not blow the chips from the aperture, as they may get into your eyes: tip them out.

Continue working on the inner surface of the aperture, keeping it as smooth as possible. As the shell walls become thinner, fix it in the vice sideways, supported on a block of scrap wood. Use the minimum of pressure to hold it, and pack the sides above the hole with wedges or thick towels so that it does not crack. Take particular care as you work on the deepest part of the hollow where there is a change of grain. It will not be easy to blend the surfaces smoothly together at this point, and if you cut too deeply from one direction, you will have to cut back the

adjacent surface.

To deepen the hollow further, change to a gouge with a deeper sweep, such as a ¼in (6mm) no. 9 or 10. A short-bladed gouge, with its corners rounded by grinding so that they do not dig into the surface, will be easier to manipulate inside the confined aperture.

When you are satisfied that the aperture is deep enough, smooth the surface by twisting the gouge and using its width to cut slightly across, but still with, the grain, as you did when working on the bowl in Chapter 8. This will allow you to remove tiny fine shavings. Remember that in a hollow, the change in grain direction will run along the deepest portion.

Scraping the inner surface

The inside of the shell can be scraped smooth with a ¼in (6mm) no. 3 gouge, provided its corners have been rounded so that they cannot scratch the surface. Alternatively, make a scraper from an old table knife, as described in Chapter 8.

The edge of the aperture should be scraped with a skew chisel, allowing tiny parings to be removed without putting too much pressure on the thin shell wall. Its shape can be altered at the same time, if required. Twist and lift the blade as you push it along, so that you use the entire length of the cutting edge, shaving over and around both inner and outer surfaces of the edge until it is completely smooth (see Fig 9.16). To round the inner portion of the edge, cut over it towards the hollow and away from the centre of the

Fig 9.16 Scrape the inside of the shell and edge of the aperture smooth.

sweep to each end of the lip. To round the outer surface, cut in the opposite direction, i.e. towards the centre of the curved outer surface. Take care to cut in the correct direction, as it is easy to remove a portion of the shell wall by accident. If this should happen, enlarge the aperture by cutting back the edge on each side of the damage, then round over the edge to finish off.

Adding the curl to the outside edge

If you look carefully at a real shell, you will see that there is a small curled channel that runs from the spiral channel around the lower half of the aperture. This is deepest

in the middle of its sweep, becoming shallower towards each end, finally blending into the outer surface of the shell.

Pencil the path of this channel on the shell, then using the skew chisel, slice sideways and scoop it out, beginning with very shallow cuts at one end and deepening them towards the middle of the curve (see Fig 9.17). Repeat from the other end of the channel to meet in the centre. The cuts are made by pushing the skew chisel forwards, at the same time twisting it so that the cutting edge is used with a scooping action. Scrape the completed channel smooth with the end of the ¼in (6mm) no. 3 gouge or the skew chisel, taking care not to work against the grain inside the hollow of the curl. Finally, blend the ends smoothly into the surface of the shell by scraping.

Completing the apex

Fasten the shell so that it is upright in the vice, using the minimum of pressure to hold it, as it could crack. To help prevent this, line the aperture with Clingfilm. Pack the aperture with Plasticine, and wrap the shell in a damp cloth to stop it from slipping.

Using the skew chisel with the same forwards slicing cut as when making the channel around the aperture, begin paring around the tip of the shell towards the apex to continue the spiral channel (as shown in Fig 9.18). Depending on the direction of the grain at this point, it may be necessary to cut in and down towards the channel. Make

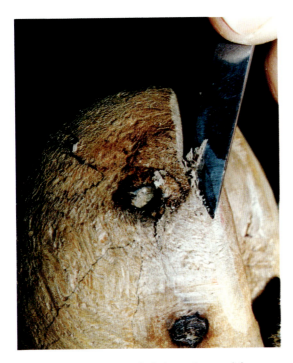

Fig 9.17 Cutting the curled channel around the aperture with a skew chisel.

sure the entire channel runs smoothly around the shell, ending almost at the tip, which should be rounded over by cutting towards the centre from all sides. Round over the remaining portion of the spiral channel, then scrape it with the skew chisel or the end of the no. 3 gouge.

Finishing

Run your hands over the shell, feeling for any irregularities or roughness, particularly inside the aperture. Mark any you find with a pencil, and remove them by paring with a no. 3 gouge, followed by scraping. Rub over all the surfaces with 240 grit garnet paper, folding it to fit inside the spiral channel and wrapping it around a piece of foam rubber to work inside the aperture. Apply a coat of cheap colourless wax polish and examine the shell for any remaining blemishes: correct them by

Fig 9.18 Completing the tip of the shell.

paring and scraping. Finally, rub over the waxed surfaces with 320 grit garnet paper to obtain a really fine finish – the abraded dust and wax will fill the pores of the wood to give a very smooth surface. Then buff with a lint-free duster. Repeat the polishing with a good quality wax polish and buff it well. Your shell is now complete.

Chapter 10

Simple Figures in the Round (i)

Standing Man

Carving figures can be fun, as there is so much inspiration to be found from people going about their daily lives. This simplified carving of a standing man, for example, is based upon the typical stance of a neighbour of mine, who likes to watch the world go by from his garden gate.

Tools you will need

- ½in (13mm) no. 3 (Swiss no. 2) gouge
- ¼in (6mm) no. 3 (Swiss no. 2) gouge
- ¼in (6mm) 60° V tool
- ¼in (6mm) skew chisel
- ¼in (6mm) no. 5 gouge (optional)
- ¼in (6mm) no. 9 gouge (optional)

Choosing and preparing the wood

For this demonstration, I chose a piece of lime, which is easy to work and illustrates the techniques well, although it is rather bland in colour. By using a more patterned wood, such as cherry or cedar, and positioning the figure carefully within the block, it would be possible to give the impression that the figure was wearing a pinstripe suit. However, if you choose this approach, be aware that the grain of the stripes may run in opposite directions in some places, and you may find it tedious to carve, although the end result will certainly be worth the effort.

As the shape of the figure is symmetrical, I used a squared block, measuring about 3in (75mm) square and 8in (200mm) long, with the grain running down its length. I split the block from a larger piece of lime, but you should be able to obtain something similar from a good timber supplier. Alternatively, you could use a

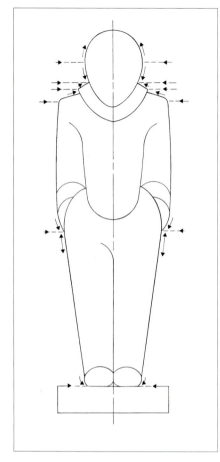

Fig 10.1 Front profile of figure.

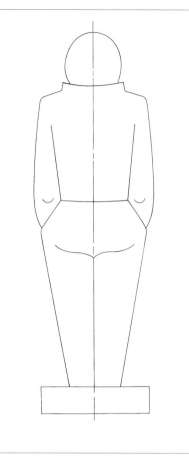

Fig 10.2 Back profile of figure.

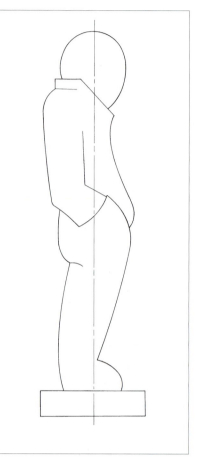

Fig 10.3 Side profile of figure.

log, about 4in (100mm) in diameter, with straight grain and no knots or flaws.

If you are not confident about drawing and placing the outlines of the figure yourself, you will find it helpful to plane the faces of the block square to each other, and draw centre-lines through each, and across the top to help you position the profiles. Make sure the base of the block is flat so that it will stand without wobbling.

Trace the front, back and side profiles, and the top view, of the figure (see Figs 10.1, 10.2, 10.3 and 10.4) and transfer them to the block, aligning the centre-lines. You can either use carbon paper to transfer the outlines directly

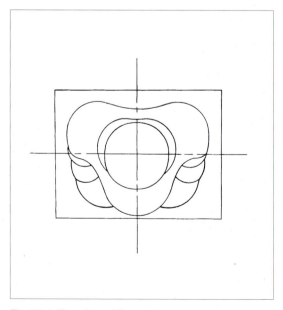

Fig 10.4 Top view of figure.

Fig 10.5 Draw the profiles on to the squared block of wood.

to the block or to copy them on to cardboard, which can be cut out to form templates. These may be taped to the block and drawn around. Flip the side tracing or template to provide left and right profiles.

If you are not confident enough to align the exterior points, such as the elbows, bottom and shoulders, by eye, you can use a try square to transfer their positions from the front view to the sides, and then to the back, provided you planed the faces of the block square as described above. Align the centre of the head from the top view with the centre-lines that run across the top of the block. This will position the figure within the block, allowing the profiles to be cut (see Fig 10.5).

Cutting the profiles

Since the figure is symmetrical in shape, and provided the block has been squared accurately, you can use a bandsaw to remove the waste from around the profiles. Remove the waste from the sides first, holding the block face up. Then temporarily replace the offcuts with double-sided tape, so that you have a side profile to work to, and remove the waste from the front and back. You will be left with a little four-sided figure.

If you do not have access to a bandsaw, you can use another method to remove the waste wood quickly. Lay the block face up and, using a pencil and try square, square lines from each projection and indent of the figure to each side of the block. Take the lines across the sides of the block and on to the back face to meet the same points on the back profile.

Fig 10.6 Make saw cuts from the edge of the block to the profile, then remove the waste with a large no. 3 gouge and mallet.

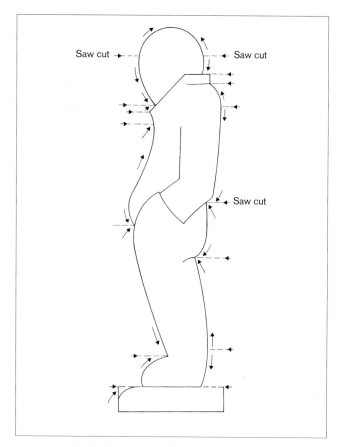

Fig 10.7 Direction of cuts for removing the waste between saw cuts.

Fig 10.8 Carve a channel beneath the sleeve and over the hips.

Holding the block with one side uppermost, saw down each line until you reach the profile on the front and back faces. Then turn it over and repeat the cuts from the other side. Use a ½in (13mm) no. 3 gouge, and mallet to remove the waste wood between the saw cuts (see Fig 10.6). The quickest way of doing this is to hold the block upright in the vice and gently split the wood downwards, holding the gouge bevel against the block so that its corners do not become embedded in the wood, thus removing small splinters. Watch carefully as you cut away the waste, stopping and reversing the direction of cut if a split appears and runs into the figure. Where you come across an indent in

the profile, split the wood back on each side to the neighbouring projection, then cut in at an angle towards the saw cut, across the width of the face (as shown in Fig 10.7).

Re-draw the centre-lines and side profiles, and repeat the process to remove the waste from the front and back faces of the block. Clean up all the surfaces and remove all evidence of the saw cuts with shallow cuts made with the ½ and ¼in (13 and 6mm) no. 3 gouges, re-drawing the necessary details, such as the outlines of the arms, the collar, etc. Finally, round off the upper edges of the base to prevent them from being broken accidentally while you are carving.

Rounding the edges

Using a ½in (13mm) no. 3 gouge with the mallet, round over the top of the feet from the front, lifting your gouge hand to remove the sharp sawn edge across the top of the toes. Reduce the size of the base if it gets in the way by splitting away small sections along the edge, remembering to round it off as before.

Round over the top of the head, working

from the top of the collar, then round under the chin, taking care not to split off the side of the head. To prevent this from happening, cut diagonally across and up at the same time, making sure the corners of the tool are clear of the wood as you cut. Using this diagonal cutting action, and following the grain direction, carefully round across the tops of the shoulders and arms, and along the outer edges of the bottom and legs as far as the heels. Here, you will have to release the chips by cutting parallel to the base.

Working from the back and across the edge of the figure, carve a channel that cuts in under the sleeve and runs up across the hips and bottom, using the ½in (13mm) no. 3 gouge to make opposing cuts. Repeat this on the other side (see Fig 10.8), then round the edges of the underside of the bottom into the top of the thigh, bringing the crease under the bottom and around the side of each leg. Shave with the gouge bevel uppermost to smooth round the sides of the hips, then cut towards the bottom from the leg side to round the sides of the thighs.

Shaping the head and collar

From the front, using the ½ or ¼in (13 or 6mm) no. 3 gouge, cut a curved channel around under the chin and back to where the ears would be, linking up with the sawn edge of the collar at the back of the head (as shown in Figs 10.9, 10.10 and 10.11). Shave away the face and head side of the channel so that the collar stands proud. Remove the projecting corners of the collar, on top of the shoulders, so that the collar fits neatly around the head. By

Fig 10.9 Begin cutting a curved channel between the chin and ears.

Fig 10.10 Make opposing cuts to complete the channel.

Fig 10.11 Continue the curved channel around to the back of the head.

cutting in towards the channel under the chin, remove the surface in front of the shoulders and collar bones to form the top of the collar, and drop the shoulders back so that there is a considerable slope down to the stomach. Round the chin into the collar, re-draw the edge of the collar on the shoulders, and mark it

Fig 10.12 (left) Outlining the collar with the V tool.

Fig 10.13 (below left) Pare away the surface below to leave the collar standing proud.

out using the V tool (see Fig 10.12). Now return to the no. 3 gouge to remove the surface below the V-cut, leaving the collar standing proud (as shown in Fig 10.13).

Working from the back of the head, around the sides to the front, form the collar into a smooth shape that flows continuously around the head. Continue to shape the sides of the head and, if necessary, reshape the top until it has a pleasing egg-shape. Then, using your widest ½in (13mm) no. 3 gouge, held bevel uppermost and with hand pressure only, smooth the head by making small slicing cuts all over the surface.

Shaping the back, elbows and bottom

Working down the back, gently scoop a triangular-shaped hollow between the shoulder blades with your ½in (13mm) no. 3 gouge, gradually rounding over each shoulder. Then extend the hollow down the spine to blend the surface with the waist, and pare all meeting surfaces clean. Re-draw the inner line of each arm, around the elbow, to join up with the channel previously cut along the edge of the sleeve. Begin at the armpit and mark the line of the arm, using the V tool, as the line will run directly along the grain. Returning to your ½in (13mm) no. 3 gouge, deepen the channels with opposing cuts (see Figs 10.14 and 10.15), and remove the area between the arms so that they

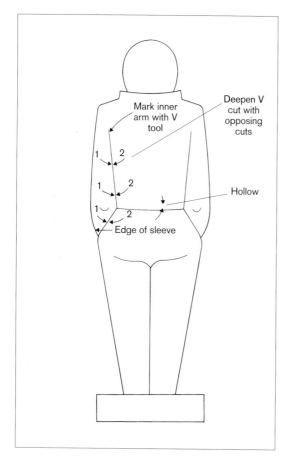

Fig 10.14 Shaping the back.

Fig 10.15 Cut channels along the inside of the arms.

Fig 10.16 Scoop a hollow across the hips.

Fig 10.17 Create a hollow in front of each arm.

are proud. Then round the edges of the arms by cutting across and into the V-channel. If necessary, use a narrower no. 3 gouge to deepen the channel near the elbows, allowing you to cut in further.

Scoop a hollow across the top of the hips, at the base of the spine, taking care not to cut into the end grain at the deepest part of the cavity (see Fig 10.16) so that you are left with a smooth surface. From each elbow, deepen the channel around the edge of the sleeve and across the hip at the side of the figure. Then pare away the surface below the sleeve, reducing the hip so that the sleeve stands out. Finally, round off the buttocks, cutting towards the upper thighs and the point where the trousers droop from the seat.

Front of the arms, paunch and pockets

Cutting up towards the shoulder, and leaving a gentle mound in the middle of the figure for the paunch, remove wood from in front of the arm. Use a ¼in (6mm) no. 5 gouge to remove the wood quickly, followed by a ¼in (6mm) no. 3 gouge to smooth the surface. Re-draw the arm and use the V tool to cut along this line,

working first towards the elbow from the sleeve, then to the armpit, and finally from the end of the sleeve towards the centre and the paunch. Deepen the channels, scooping out hollows in front of the bent elbow and along the length of the forearm and upper arm, using the no. 5 gouge (see Fig 10.17). Stop when the wood begins to split. Now form a crease across the bend of the elbow, cutting outwards with the no. 3 gouge, and working into this channel to produce a deep triangular hollow where the side of the torso meets the arm (see Figs 10.18, 10.19 and 10.20). Repeat this for the other side of the figure, then round off the arms.

You can give the paunch as rounded a shape as you like, making it overhang the waist by cutting a curved V-channel beneath it and removing wood from the waist/crotch area using the ½ or ¼in (13 or 6mm) gouge. To form the pockets, shave a continuous surface from below and to the side of the paunch to the forearm. Then cut a V-channel, making

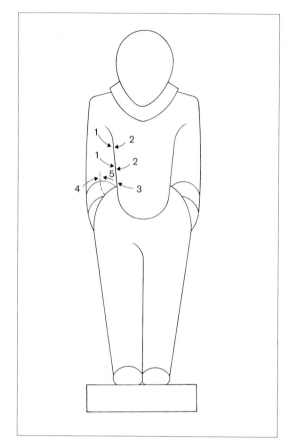

Fig 10.18 Shaping the arm and paunch.

Fig 10.19 Create a triangular hollow where the torso meets the arm.

channel. Round over the inside edges of the feet, cutting towards and across the ankles so that the two channels join neatly. Repeat the process for the back of the legs and the area between the heels. Here, you will be able to cut

opposing cuts using the ¼in (6mm) no. 3 gouge, around the end of the sleeve towards the paunch. Reduce the surface of the sleeve so that the edge of the pocket stands up in front of it, repeating the process for the other pocket.

The legs

At the front of the figure, cut with the V tool straight down between the legs, from crotch to ankles. Then make another V-cut in the end grain between the feet, from the toes towards the ankles, joining the two channels. Round over the edges of the legs with the no. 3 gouge, using it bevel uppermost, if necessary, near the ankles to place the corner of the blade into the

Fig 10.20 Shape the paunch to overhang the waist and flow around into the arms.

straight down to the base with the V tool and detach the chip using the corner of the gouge. Reduce the width of the heels a little, so that the feet are wider across the toes, and very slightly undercut the edges of the shoes on the base. If you want to show the ends of the trousers, cut a V-channel around each ankle and pare away the surface of the ankle beneath, allowing the trouser legs to stand out above the shoes.

Finishing

Inspect all the edges and angles between adjoining surfaces of the carving, looking for any stray cuts, nicks or wood fibres. Remove any you find with the ¼in (6mm) no. 3 gouge and the ¼in (6mm) skew chisel, as appropriate. Pay particular attention to features that run along the grain, such as the channels between the legs and along the inner arms, and at the bottoms of hollows, such as the small of the back, where a change in cutting direction was required. Tidy up the edges of the base, altering its shape if you wish. Then, using a deep gouge, such as a ¼in (6mm) no. 9 or no. 5, carefully make a series of even cuts all over it to provide a texture that contrasts with the figure.

If you have chosen a well patterned piece of wood, take advantage of this and finish the figure by scraping all the surfaces smooth, in the direction of the grain, using a cabinet scraper. Scrape into the confined areas with the edge of your no. 3 gouge or the skew chisel. Apply a coat of cheap colourless wax with an old toothbrush, leave it to soak in for a while, then rub the carving smooth with 240 or 320 grit garnet paper to produce a fine finish. The abraded dust will combine with the wax to fill the pores of the wood, leaving a very smooth surface that will enhance the pattern of the grain. Finally, apply a good quality wax polish, buffing it well with a lint-free duster.

While you can treat a bland wood, such as that used for this demonstration, in a similar manner, it can be given a more interesting surface by tooling. I used a ½in (13mm) no. 3 gouge, but a no. 4 or no. 5 would also be suitable. Having sharpened the tool beforehand, so that each cut you make is smooth and burnished, carefully make shallow cuts over the entire surface to give clean facets that will reflect the light when the carving is polished. Do not use any abrasive afterwards, as this will soften the facets and spoil the tooled surface. You can either tool the base in the same way, or leave it smooth to contrast with the figure. I favour using Danish oil on a wood such as this, as it brings out the colour. It was applied with a brush, the excess wiped off, and then left to soak in overnight. Finally, the figure was polished with a good quality wax and a piece of felt glued to the base.

You will notice from the photographs that my carving developed a large crack in the head, but I filled this successfully by taking slivers of wood from the base, coating them with glue and packing them tightly into the crack so that their grain direction corresponded with that of the carving. Having allowed the glue to dry overnight, I shaved off the ends of the slivers, and the surface around the crack, with a no. 3 gouge, used by hand. The result was a repair that is hardly noticeable.

Chapter 11

Simple Figures in the Round (ii)

Sitting Man

This simple abstract figure requires all the basic techniques learned in Chapters 6, 7 and 8: rounding as used for the hedgehog; opposing-cut channel cutting, such as that employed on the heron in relief; and the hollowing, scraping and finishing methods carried out on the bowl.

Tools you will need

- 1in (25mm) no. 3 (Swiss no. 2) gouge
- ½in (13mm) no. 9 gouge
- ½in (13mm) no. 5 gouge
- ½in (13mm) no. 3 (Swiss no. 2) gouge
- ¼in (6mm) no. 3 (Swiss no. 2) gouge
- ¼in (6mm) no. 5 gouge
- ⅛in (3mm) no. 3 (Swiss no. 2) gouge
- ¼in (6mm) 60° V tool
- ¼in (6mm) skew chisel
- Surform
- Convex-soled spokeshave (optional)
- Cabinet scraper
- Table knife scraper, ground with a rounded end (optional)

Choosing and preparing the wood

Any of the fruit woods would be ideal for this project, being lovely to carve. I chose a half log of pear, making use of the rounded portion for the curved back of the figure, and the grain lengthwise from base to head. The original log was about 6in (150mm) in diameter, and I cut a section from it measuring about 6in (150mm) long, splitting it in half with an axe. Then with the 1in (25mm) no. 3 gouge and mallet, I cleared away the bark until the surface was sound. I used the same gouge to smooth the split face sufficiently to be able to draw on it. You could use a squared block instead, but before you begin carving in earnest, the portion that will form the back of the figure must be rounded off like a log. Whatever you use, make sure the ends are cut parallel to each other so that the wood can be held in the vice easily.

Basic shaping

Transfer the front view of the figure (see Fig 11.1) to the flat face of the wood in the normal manner, using tracing and carbon paper. If you feel confident enough, you can draw the shape freehand, which would allow you to elongate or shorten the figure if you want to use a piece of wood of a different size. You will see that the top corners, above the shoulders, need removing so that the head forms the highest point. Note that this is *offset* slightly to one side to give the impression of a slouch. Remove the corners of the wood with a ½in (13mm) no. 9 gouge and mallet, rounding them so that they curve up towards the top of the head when viewed from the front (see Fig 11.2).

Now round over the back by cutting *towards* the top of the head, starting at the edge of the log and lifting your gouge hand as you round it over, as you did when shaping the rear end of the hedgehog in Chapter 6. Work along the sides to meet the curve of the shoulders, shaping the wood so that the rounded surface begins at about halfway along its length. This is a little above the point at which the bench will be formed (see Figs 11.1 and 11.3). Leave a

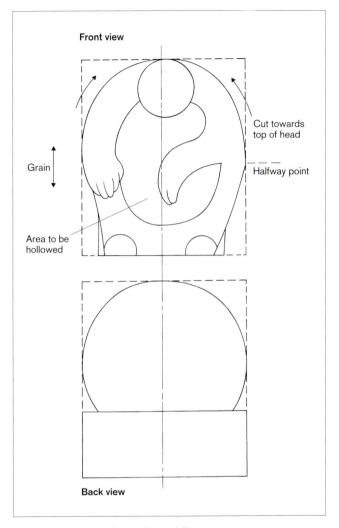

Fig 11.1 Front and back views of figure.

Fig 11.2 Round the corners of the wood towards the top of the head.

Fig 11.3 Rounding the back of the figure.

small flat area at the top of the head so that you can still hold the wood in the vice without difficulty. When you have achieved a pleasing shape, which need not be symmetrical, smooth the surface with the 1in (25mm) no. 3 gouge or a Surform until it feels comfortable in your hands. At this point, you are ready to begin carving the features.

Beginning the hollow

On the flat face of the wood, use the V tool and mallet to cut around the outline of the head, the inner edges of both arms, and across the knees, which is the area to be hollowed. Then cut around the tops of the feet and along the outer edge of each leg, from elbow to base. Be sure to cut in the correct direction, i.e. *with* the grain, changing where necessary to prevent the wood from splitting. Now enlarge the V-channel around the hollow, using your no. 3 gouges and the opposing-cut method described in Chapter 7 for outlining the heron (see Fig 11.4). Continue until the channel is about ¼in (6mm) deep and wide. Then draw a line across the area to be hollowed to mark the deepest area, as you did when hollowing the bowl in Chapter 8. This part of carving the figure can be regarded as simply hollowing an oddly-shaped bowl, as the techniques are exactly the same.

Cut into the waste wood from each side of the line, using a ½in (13mm) no. 9 or no. 5 gouge and a mallet, deepening the hollow until the rim begins to get in the way (as shown in Fig 11.5). When this occurs, round over the edge so that you can continue, but do not

Fig 11.4 Enlarging the channel around the central hollow.

Fig 11.5 Deepening the hollow.

undercut the rim. Round over the edge of the chin: it may be necessary to reshape this as you deepen the chest hollow. Continue in this way until the hollow is ½–¾in (13–19mm) deep at its lowest point, where you may find it easier to scoop out the wood by hand. Although it will be necessary to deepen the hollow further at a later stage, for now, tidy the surface so that it is reasonably smooth. Then you are ready to move on to the next step.

Shaping the head and setting back the shoulders

Draw on the centre-line of the head, then use the ½in (13mm) no. 3 gouge and mallet to round over the sharp edge of the V-cut that outlines the head, and remove the adjacent surfaces of the shoulders so that the head projects a little from them (see Fig 11.6). Re-cut the V-channel until it is about ¼in (6mm)

Fig 11.7 Cutting back the shoulders.

Fig 11.8 Rounding over the top and sides of the head.

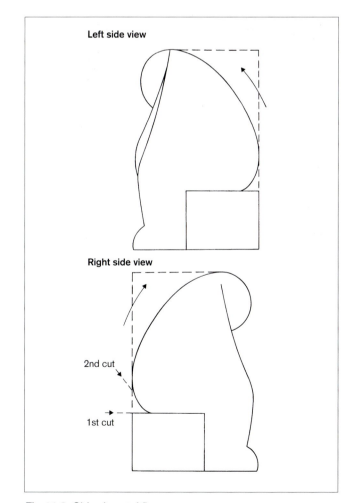

Fig 11.6 Side views of figure.

Left side view

Right side view

2nd cut

1st cut

deep, making opposing cuts with the no. 3 gouge and remembering to turn the gouge to match the curve of cut required. Using a deeper gouge, such as a ½in (13mm) no. 5 or no. 9, remove the surface of the shoulders until it is level with the bottom of the channel (see Fig 11.7), providing a substantial slope back from wrists to shoulders (as shown in Fig 11.6). When working near the head, tilt the gouge slightly so that its corner will remove the edge of the channel without cutting into the head itself. Then round over the top and sides of the head again (see Fig 11.8).

To round the lower part of the head, re-cut the V-channel, working *towards* the centre-line from each side. You can use the V tool here, as you will be working along the grain and in end grain (see Fig 11.9). Again, round over the sharp edges left by the V tool by sweeping the tilted no. 3 gouge around the side of the head towards the centre-line (see Fig 11.10). Repeat for the other side of the head until it is completely rounded from top to bottom and across the centre.

The rounded surface of the head should be continued into the hollowed chest, and some undercutting will be needed across the chin: tilt the no. 3 gouge underneath it and scoop out the wood, so cutting with the grain (see Fig 11.11). Open up the hollow on each side by scooping from each side of the chin and the edges of the shoulders, twisting the tool at the same time as pushing it around the hollow.

You will find that as the surfaces of the shoulders and arms are removed, the width of the hollowed chest will diminish and the arms will become wider. They should be restored to their former sizes by widening and deepening the hollow further.

The legs and feet

Turn the carving on each side in turn, then, with the ½in (13mm) no. 5 or no. 3 gouge, work from elbow to base to remove the wedge-shaped area beyond the outer edge of the leg, so that the elbows are the widest part of the figure when viewed from the front. In the process, remove the outer portions of the V-channels outlining the legs and ensure that the sides of the feet flow into the sides of the legs.

Next, deepen the V-channel that runs over the top and down the inside of each foot, making opposing cuts with the ¼in (6mm) no. 3 gouge and removing about ¼in (6mm) from between the feet and under the hand to leave

Fig 11.9 Cutting a V-channel around the lower portion of the head.

Fig 11.10 Round over the sharp edges of the V-channel.

Fig 11.11 Undercut the area of the chin.

Fig 11.12 Shaping the feet.

Fig 11.13 Forming the top surface of the bench.

Fig 11.14 Remove wood from the side of the leg so that the bench projects.

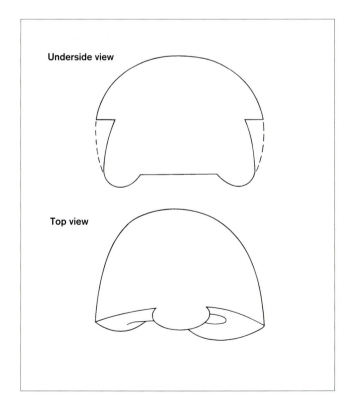

Underside view

Top view

the feet projecting (as shown in Fig 11.12). Round over the tops of the feet and slightly chamfer the soles so that they cannot break off. Finally, cutting towards the fingertips, slope the surface of the figure's right hand from the knuckles to the fingertips, and over the side of the hollow, where the thumb will lie, in preparation for carving the fingers.

Forming the bench

At about a third of the height of the carving, from the bottom, draw the horizontal top edge of the bench across the back and sides of the figure. Draw the vertical ends of the bench about 1in (25mm) back from the front of the figure. Using the ½in (13mm) no. 3 gouge, make opposing cuts across the grain to form the top edges of the bench and round the rear of the figure into its upper surface (see Figs 11.6 and 11.13). Deepen these cuts until the bench top projects about ½in (13mm) from the rear and sides of the figure. Pare the surface smooth and remove any deep cuts or nicks.

Using the V tool, cut a deep channel along the vertical line at each end of the bench, and remove the wood from alongside the leg, in front of the bench with the ¼in (6mm) no. 5 or no. 3 gouge (see Fig 11.14). The side of the bench should project about ¼in (6mm) from the leg (as shown in Fig 11.15), while the surface of each leg should flow smoothly to the shoulder. Tidy the edges of the bench and the areas of the figure that touch it. Alter the curve of the shoulders to the top of the head so that the figure feels comfortable in your hands. Then remove any marks left by the Surform, using a

Fig 11.15 Top and bottom views of figure.

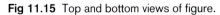

139

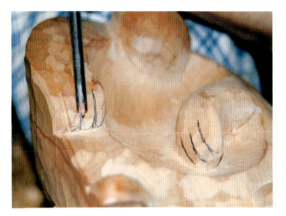

Fig 11.16 Cutting between the fingers with the V tool.

large no. 3 gouge, bevel downwards, by hand or a convex-soled spokeshave, as described for the hedgehog project in Chapter 6.

Finishing the hollow

Returning to the front of the figure, deepen and widen the hollow until its shape approximately corresponds to that of the back, using your fingers to gauge any differences. Form each hand into a smooth spatula shape with rounded edges. Use a ¼in (6mm) no. 5 gouge, by hand, to pare the slope beneath the figure's left hand so that it flows smoothly into the rest of the hollow. Undercut the arm and the chin-to-neck areas, and smooth the upper surface of the arm into the hollow, again by hand, tilting and scooping forwards with the ¼in (6mm) no. 3 gouge. Finally, run your fingers over the hollow, feeling for any irregularities or roughness. Remove these by scraping with the ¼in (6mm) no. 3 gouge or a homemade table knife scraper, as you did for the bowl in Chapter 8.

The hands

Draw the fingers on each hand, then use the V tool to cut channels between the fingers (as shown in Fig 11.16). Round the sides of the fingers with the ⅛in (3mm) no. 3 gouge, held bevel uppermost. With the ⅛in (3mm) no. 3 gouge, shorten the little finger and thumb on the outside of each hand, then round under the tips and scrape them smooth (the point of a skew chisel can be used to scrape between the fingers).

Tidying and finishing

Examine all surfaces where they meet, making sure that there is no raggedness in the angles. Then scrape the bench, the surface between the feet, the arms and the head with the cabinet scraper, or the end of a ¼in (6mm) no. 3 gouge. Because the pear wood I used was rather uniform in colour, for contrast, I tooled the back of the figure, using shallow cuts from a ½in (13mm) no. 3 gouge. However, just as effective would have been to tool the front of the figure, leaving the back and the bench smooth. A more patterned wood might have benefited from being left completely smooth.

To finish, I applied a coat of cheap colourless wax polish and rubbed the whole figure with 320 grit garnet paper. The wax and abraded dust not only filled the pores in the wood, but also the worm hole visible in Fig 11.11, leaving a very smooth surface. Finally, to bring out the colour of the wood, Danish oil was applied and left to dry, after which the carving was treated with good quality wax and buffed with a lint-free duster.

Chapter 12

Using Contrasts

Birds

All woods differ in colour and grain pattern, and one of the exciting aspects of carving is that the appearance of these changes constantly as you shape the wood. You can use these qualities to turn simple tactile shapes into attractive carvings that do not require much detailing, as shown by this group of birds, which make good use of the contrasting heart- and sapwood in a forked yew branch. You will notice that as carving progresses, the shapes and proportions of the birds can be altered, making it a flexible and enjoyable piece to work on.

Tools you will need

- ½in (13mm) no. 9 gouge
- ½in (13mm) no. 5 gouge
- ½in (13mm) no. 3 (Swiss no. 2) gouge
- ¼in (6mm) no. 9 gouge
- ¼in (6mm) no. 5 gouge
- ¼in (6mm) no. 3 gouge
- ¼in (6mm) 60° V tool
- ¼in (6mm) skew chisel
- ⅛in (3mm) no. 9, no. 10 or no. 11 gouge
- Mallet
- Surform
- Cabinet scraper

Choosing and preparing the wood

Once your friends and family know that you have taken up carving, you are likely to receive a variety of pieces and branches of wood that they think may be useful to you. Although carvers accustomed to working with squared blocks may discard such gifts, many will be worth keeping, as with imagination they can often be turned into interesting carvings. Such was the case with the crotch of yew shown in this chapter. It was irregular in shape, having three branches and a main trunk measuring about 5in (125mm) in diameter.

The heartwood of this particular piece of yew was orange-brown in colour, although it can be darker, while the sapwood was creamy white. With careful thought, the contrast between the two colours can be used to good effect, as it was in this project. I use the techniques shown here extensively in my own carvings. Not much detail is necessary in the

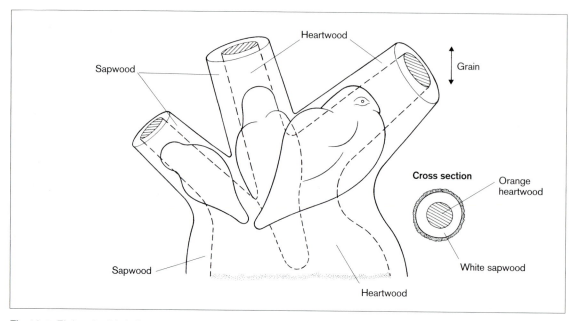

Fig 12.1 Fitting the birds into a crotch of wood.

carvings, since the grain pattern of yew is always interesting: the birds can be given a smooth finish, with a tooled base for added interest. Other woods with similar colour contrasts, which could be used in the same way, are plum, cedar, laburnum and walnut.

The main trunk of the crotch was sawn to about 4in (100mm) in length, and the base flattened with the Surform, which was fitted with a flat blade. The branches were shortened to the

Fig 12.2 Mark the direction in which each bird faces.

height of the birds (see Fig 12.1), while the bark was carefully removed with shallow cuts from a 1in (25mm) no. 3 gouge and mallet, leaving as much of the white sapwood as possible.

Carving the birds

The direction in which each bird was to face was marked with an arrow (see Fig 12.2). Then the top of each was rounded over with the ½in (13mm) no. 9 gouge and a mallet, lifting the handle of the tool to make a rounded cut and working around each branch until no sharp or sawn edges remained. This is the same technique as used for carving the hedgehog in Chapter 6.

The two adjacent birds were separated, from a point above their wings, by cutting towards the top of each head with the ¼in (6mm) no. 9 gouge and mallet, removing a wedge-shaped section of wood between them. The heads were rounded with the Surform, while the back of each bird was given a slope

Fig 12.3 The back of each bird is made to slope from head to tail.

from head to tail with the ½in (13mm) no. 5 gouge, as shown in Fig 12.3. Then the heads were narrowed with the same tool to give shape to the tops of the wings.

The bodies and tails

The back of each bird was smoothed with the ½in (13mm) no. 3 gouge, then a channel was cut around the tail and body, using the opposing-cut method outlined in previous chapters. The edges of the body and tail were shaped into the channel (see Fig 12.4). By repeating these steps, each bird was gradually rounded under from its breast to the tail, and the perch formed (see Fig 12.5). In the process, the sapwood was gradually removed, leaving the heartwood as the surface of the breast. I did not think it necessary to carve feet, but a small area could have been left for refining into toes later, using the techniques shown in Chapter 7 for the heron.

I thought that the birds looked a little too upright, so I sawed a wedge-shaped section from the base of the carving to tilt the entire piece slightly forwards. This is quite a useful technique, but it must be used with care, for if

Fig 12.4 (top) Shaping the edges of the body and tail.

Fig 12.5 (below) Round under the bodies of the birds and shape the top of the perch.

too much wood is removed, the carving may become unsteady. To determine how much wood to remove, place a piece of scrap wood beneath one edge to tilt the carving in the desired direction and by the required amount. Then measure the distance from the raised edge to the bench and transfer this measurement to the edge directly opposite. From this point, remove the wedge of wood so that it tapers to nothing at the far edge. Finally, smooth the base again with the Surform.

Fig 12.6 Reduce the heads and upper bodies of the birds.

The heads and upper bodies of the adjacent pair of birds were reduced further (see Fig 12.6), increasing the space between them. Since this would have involved cutting into end grain if gouges had been used, an initial V-channel was cut between the birds (see Fig 12.7) with the ¼in (6mm) V tool. By tilting the corner of the ¼in (6mm) no. 5 gouge (a no. 3 gouge would have worked, too), each side of the channel could be rounded away from the bottom towards the top of each wing.

The channel outlining the tails was deepened, using the ½in (13mm) no. 3 gouge with opposing cuts, and the surface of the perch, below the tails, was then removed by cutting into the channel with the ¼in (6mm) no. 5 gouge. Repeating these cuts several times, slightly increasing the amount of undercutting, resulted in the tails standing proud. The single bird now appeared to have grown taller, so it was reduced in size and reshaped until it was in proportion again, using the methods outlined above.

Next, the birds were smoothed and made anatomically symmetrical, a centre-line being drawn on each for reference. The work was done with the ½in (13mm) no. 3 gouge, used by hand with the bevel uppermost, slicing cuts being made around the shape to smooth any ridges left by the deeper gouges. In this way, the shapes were adjusted until they were pleasing to the touch. The angles where the birds and perch met were pared smooth using the ½ and ¼in (13 and 6mm) no. 3 gouges, as well as the skew chisel in confined spaces.

Fig 12.7 Separating the birds.

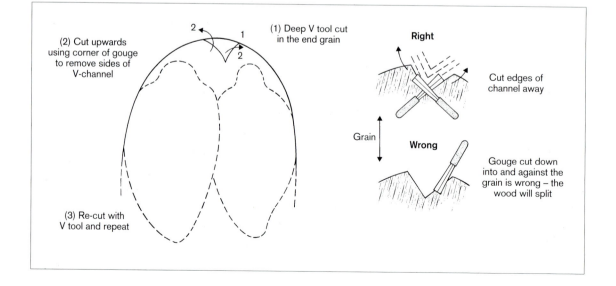

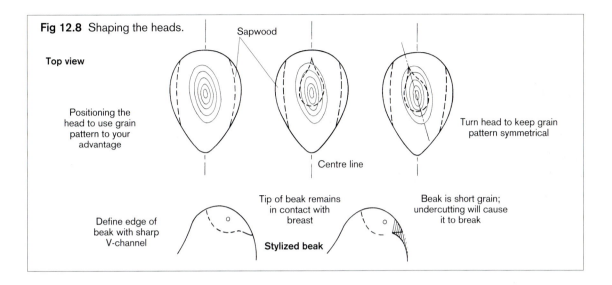

Fig 12.8 Shaping the heads.

Top view

Sapwood

Positioning the head to use grain pattern to your advantage

Centre line

Turn head to keep grain pattern symmetrical

Define edge of beak with sharp V-channel

Tip of beak remains in contact with breast

Stylized beak

Beak is short grain; undercutting will cause it to break

The heads

The outline of the head and beak (a teardrop shape) was drawn on the highest point of each bird (the crown of the head), the tip of the beak being set back from the breast when viewed from above, with the grain pattern symmetrical (see Fig 12.8). The ¼in (6mm) no. 9 gouge was used to cut a channel around the outline, giving it a soft edge, and the tops of the wings pared into the channel with the ¼in (6mm) no. 5 gouge (as shown in Fig 12.9). Above the channel, the head was narrowed and rounded up towards the crown with the same tool, then smoothed by

hand with the ½in (13mm) no. 3 gouge, held bevel uppermost. The angle of the back of the head was altered slightly to emerge smoothly from between the wings (see Fig 12.10).

The beaks of carved birds are often vulnerable, being positioned so that they are short-grained and likely to break easily. This problem was overcome by stylizing the beak and lowering the tip to touch the breast, as if the bird was dozing (see Fig 12.8). Paring by hand with the ¼in (6mm) no. 3 gouge, the tip of the beak was reduced and its sides angled so that the apex sloped up towards the crown of the head. Each side of the beak was redefined

Fig 12.9 Shaping the tops of the wings.

Fig 12.10 Adjusting the angle of the back of the head.

Fig 12.11 Removing the sapwood from the perch.

by cutting a shallow groove alongside it with the ⅛in (3mm) no. 9 gouge (although a no. 10 or no. 11 gouge would have worked equally well) and removing a little of the adjacent surface of the breast with the ¼in (6mm) no. 3 gouge. The shape and position of each head were carefully adjusted to give a symmetrical grain pattern on top, paring by hand with the ½in (13mm) no. 3 gouge, held bevel uppermost.

Finally, the birds were scraped smooth with the cabinet scraper, using the edge of the ¼in (6mm) no. 3 gouge and the skew chisel to scrape in confined areas of the carving.

The perch

Using the ½in (13mm) no. 5 gouge and mallet, the white sapwood on the perch (beneath the tail of each bird) was removed until the darker heartwood showed clearly to contrast with the lighter colour of the birds (see Fig 12.11).

For added interest, I decided to carve ivy leaves in relief on the perch to demonstrate how you can use the sapwood for leaves that contrast with a background of orange heartwood.

In the area where the sapwood was thickest (seen from beneath the base), I drew a few ivy leaves on the surface. As when carving the heron in Chapter 7, the leaves were outlined with the V tool, and that outline deepened by cutting in with appropriate sizes of no. 3 gouge. The adjacent sapwood was removed completely to leave a contrasting background of the dark heartwood. Each leaf was modelled to give it an undulating surface, its centre vein being cut as a fold, while the edges were undercut as necessary. They were finished by scraping the surface smooth with the end of the ¼in (6mm) no. 3 gouge and the skew chisel. The main stem was not carved, but its line could have been incised with the V tool.

The rest of the sapwood was removed from the perch, and the surface of the exposed heartwood carefully tooled with a ¼in (6mm) no. 5 gouge to contrast with the smooth surface of the birds.

Finishing

Having initially drawn open eyes on the birds, I decided that they would look better half closed, so the lids were shown as crescent-shaped grooves. These were cut with the ⅛in (3mm) no. 9 gouge, although a no. 10 or no. 11 gouge or a V tool could have been used instead. I wanted the curves to taper in width towards each end, so the depth of cut was reduced at the ends.

Each bird was given a coat of cheap, colourless wax polish, applied with an old toothbrush and allowed to soak in for a while. Then the waxed surfaces were abraded with 320 grit garnet paper, giving the birds a very smooth finish in contrast to the textured surface of the perch. Finally, the entire carving was treated with good quality wax polish and buffed with a lint-free duster. A piece of felt was glued to the base.

Chapter 13

Deep Relief
and Undercutting
Bird Feeder

By using the techniques demonstrated in the previous chapters, you will be able to make a range of carvings that are not only decorative, but also functional, which can make delightful personalized gifts for friends and family. A good example is the bird feeder shown in this chapter, which is attractively decorated with relief carvings. The design is quite versatile: if enlarged, given a deeper hollow and some drainage holes, it would make a useful planter.

Tools you will need

- ¾in (19mm) no. 3 (Swiss no. 2) gouge
- ½in (13mm) no. 3 (Swiss no. 2) gouge
- ¼in (6mm) no. 3 (Swiss no. 2) gouge
- ⅛in (3mm) no. 3 (Swiss no. 2) gouge
- ½in (13mm) no. 9 gouge
- ½in (13mm) no. 5 gouge
- ¼in (6mm) no. 5 gouge
- ¼in (6mm) skew chisel
- ¼in (6mm) 60° V tool
- Mallet
- Surform
- Cabinet scraper

Choosing and preparing the wood

I used a quartered log of sycamore for this project, measuring approximately 10in (254mm) long by about 6in (150mm) wide and deep. Most of the woods listed in the glossary on page 175 could be used for this, but oak, elm or any of the fruit woods would be particularly suitable. The size is not critical: you could make it larger or smaller if you wish.

The back of the feeder, which would be mounted against a wall, was planed smooth and the bark removed from the rest of the wood, using a 1in (25mm) no. 3 (Swiss no. 2) gouge and mallet. The outer corners of the log were sawn off, then the ends were rounded over by making cuts with the ½in (13mm) no. 9 gouge, followed by the ½in (13mm) no. 5 gouge, both being used with a mallet. The

Fig 13.1 Round the corners of the wood with no. 9 and no. 5 gouges, then smooth it with a Surform.

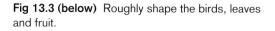

Fig 13.2 (top) The relief design was drawn on the feeder and outlined in the normal manner.

Fig 13.3 (below) Roughly shape the birds, leaves and fruit.

remaining ridges were smoothed with the Surform until the carving felt comfortable to hold (see Fig 13.1). At this stage, I found it helpful to write 'back' and 'top' on the appropriate surfaces to avoid confusion.

Next, I drew a rim on the top face, about ½in (13mm) from the edge. A smooth hollow was created inside this line to a depth of about ½in (13mm), using the techniques described in Chapter 8 for hollowing the bowl. The inner and outer edges of the rim were rounded over with the ½in (13mm) no. 5 and no. 3 gouges.

Carving the exterior

A deep relief design of birds and leaves is appropriate for a feeder, and this was drawn on the rounded surface, the leaves being overlapped so that no empty spaces were left (see Fig 13.2). A common mistake when carving leaves is to arrange them in a random manner, as separate items with their top surfaces too flat, instead of overlapping and twisting them in sprays around the shape of the wood. To add contrast and reduce the number of leaves, which can become tedious to carve if there are too many, several apples were added.

The design was carved using the techniques described for relief carving in Chapter 7. First it was outlined with the ¼in (6mm) V tool, then the channels were deepened and widened with a selection of no. 3 gouges before establishing the levels of the various parts of the design. The birds, leaves and apples were then shaped using a selection of widths of no. 3 gouges (see Fig 13.3). The depth of carving is

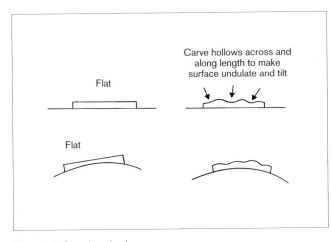

Fig 13.4 Shaping the leaves.

Fig 13.5 Scrape the apples, birds and leaves smooth, then carve the detail.

a matter of choice, but deeper cuts will provide you with more scope for shaping. In places, my cuts were over ½in (13mm) deep, providing plenty of room to overlap the leaves, shape the birds and round the apples.

Each leaf was given an undulating surface, the edges being tilted or rounded as required (see Fig 13.4). At this stage, it is important not to undercut the edges, otherwise they may collapse while you are still working on them. The apples and birds were scraped smooth (see Fig 13.5), and the detail carved on the birds with the V tool and the ¼ or ⅛in (6 or 3mm) no. 3 gouges. Finally, the leaves were scraped smooth, and all angles between surfaces cut clean and tidied, using the ⅛ and ¼in (3 and 6mm) no. 3 gouges and the skew chisel.

Next, the veins of the leaves were drawn and cut with the V tool. Curving the main leaf vein and using a few quick, short, curved strokes to mark the minor veins will give fluidity to a carving, which would be lacking if ponderous straight lines were carved with deliberation. This is another common mistake. Having cut the central vein, where

the grain allowed, the remaining veins were cut away from the centre, reducing the depth of each cut towards the edge of the leaf so that the vein tapered and ended in a point.

At this stage, the undercutting was carried out. Where the upper surface of a leaf rose, the edge was thick and heavy. This needed undercutting to produce the shadow that would make the leaf look as though it was rising (see Fig 13.6). Using the ⅛in (3mm) no. 3 gouge, the edges of the leaves were undercut as necessary, leaving the angles between the undercutting and the adjacent surfaces as tidy as possible. To add a little variation, some of the leaves were serrated by making tiny nicks along their edges with the V tool (as shown in Fig 13.6).

Finishing

The finished carving was treated with raw linseed oil, applied with a brush into the crevices, although teak or Danish oil would have

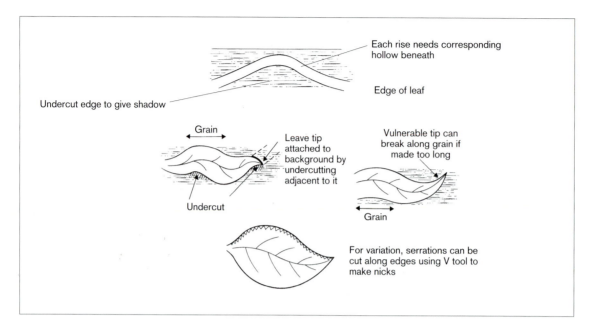

Each rise needs corresponding hollow beneath

Edge of leaf

Undercut edge to give shadow

Grain

Leave tip attached to background by undercutting adjacent to it

Vulnerable tip can break along grain if made too long

Undercut

Grain

For variation, serrations can be cut along edges using V tool to make nicks

Fig 13.6 Undercutting the edges of the leaves.

Fig 13.7 The finished bird feeder.

been as effective, and can be re-applied each year to combat weathering. I screwed two plate hangers to the back of the feeder so that it could be hung on the wall. Fastened above the workshop window and topped up with scraps, it was soon found by the local sparrows.

Chapter 14

Carving a Composition
Child and Sheep

This project is an arrangement of separately carved pieces, made entirely from small offcuts left over from other carvings. Compositions of this kind make an interesting change to working on a single, larger piece of wood, and they have the advantage that they can be added to, altered or repositioned as you wish. Although the figure of the child was carved in great detail for this demonstration, it could be left simple. All the techniques required have been used in previous chapters, so they should present you with no problems.

Choosing and preparing the wood

All the pieces were made from offcuts of lime, but any of the close-grained woods listed in the glossary on page 175 would be suitable, provided the grain was straight. Pruned tree branches would also be usable.

The sheep are carved from wedge-shaped

Tools you will need

- 1in (25mm) no. 3 (Swiss no. 2) gouge
- ½in (13mm) no. 3 (Swiss no. 2) gouge
- ¼in (6mm) no. 3 (Swiss no. 2) gouge
- ⅛in (3mm) no. 3 (Swiss no. 2) gouge
- ¹⁄₁₆in (2mm) no. 3 (Swiss no. 2) gouge
- ½in (13mm) no. 9 gouge
- ½in (13mm) no. 5 gouge
- ¼in (6mm) no. 5 gouge
- ¹⁄₁₆in (2mm) no. 5 gouge
- ¼in (6mm) no. 6 gouge (optional)
- ⅛in (3mm) no. 10 or no. 11 gouge
- ¼in (6mm) 60° V tool
- ⅛in (3mm) 60° V tool
- ¼in (6mm) skew chisel
- Mallet
- Surform
- Cabinet scraper
- Saw
- Hacksaw
- Nail (or punch) and light hammer (optional)

blocks with the grain running lengthwise, being about 2in (50mm) at the widest part of the wedge, and 3in (75mm) long. Flatten the wider end of each wedge with the Surform to act as a base, and split off the narrow tip along the grain with an axe and hammer. The child requires a piece about 6in (150mm) long by 3in (75mm) square, again with the grain running lengthwise, and the ends cut square.

Carving the sheep

Round off each block along its length, then round the ends in the same manner as the hedgehog in Chapter 6, using the ½in (13mm) no. 9 and no. 5 gouges and the mallet. Smooth the ridges left by the gouges with the Surform, giving the animal's back a slope away from the head, and rounding the underside slightly until it feels comfortable in the hand (as shown in Fig 14.1).

Draw the face and ears of each sheep on to its block, varying the position from animal to animal, and outline these with the ¼in (6mm) V tool. As in relief carving, remove the wood from around the face and ears with the ¼in (6mm) no. 5 gouge, cutting outwards and with the grain (as shown in Fig 14.2). Deepen the channel along the sides of the head and beneath the chin with the V tool, and repeat the paring process until the head stands proud. Round the head with the ¼in (6mm) no. 3 gouge, pare it to shape by hand, and smooth it ready for the facial features to be added (see Figs 14.1 and 14.3).

Fig 14.3 Continue paring around the head until it stands proud, then smooth it prior to adding the features.

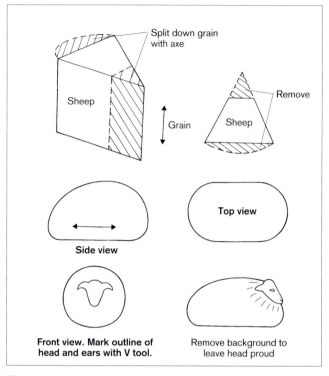

Fig 14.1 Details of the sheep.

Fig 14.2 Shaping the head of the sheep.

Fig 14.4 Texturing the sheep.

Since carving the facial features will mean working in end grain, they can be cut with the little hook that develops at the angle of the V tool blade, or by using the point of the skew chisel. The eyes are denoted by small curved nicks, and the nose by a Y-shaped cut leading to the mouth, which should be cut in from each side to meet in the centre. Ear slits can also be cut if you wish. Finally, scrape the face smooth with the end of the ¼in (6mm) no. 3 gouge and the edge of the skew chisel.

Next, the sheep need texturing, but practise the technique first on scrap wood, preferably of the same type as that used for the sheep. Hold a small, deeply curved gouge, such as a ⅛in (3mm) no. 10 or no. 11, at a steep angle to the surface of the wood and cut downwards until the corners of the blade are just clear of the surface (see Fig 14.4). While continuing to press downwards, swing the tool from side to side and push it forwards with one hand, while preventing it from slipping with your other hand (as shown in Fig 14.5). This should produce a convoluted, wiggly line with raised edges. Experiment by cutting a series of parallel lines with different depths and lengths until you feel confident enough to tackle a sheep.

As when texturing the hedgehog, draw guide lines over the sheep's body before beginning. Start cutting from each end before filling in the sides. Do not scrape or sand the textured surface, as this will remove the 'wool' effect.

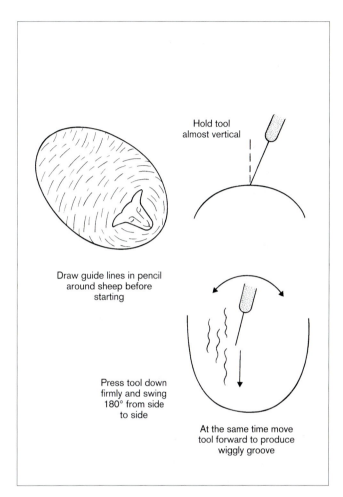

Hold tool almost vertical

Draw guide lines in pencil around sheep before starting

Press tool down firmly and swing 180° from side to side

At the same time move tool forward to produce wiggly groove

Fig 14.5 Use both hands to control the gouge when adding texture.

153

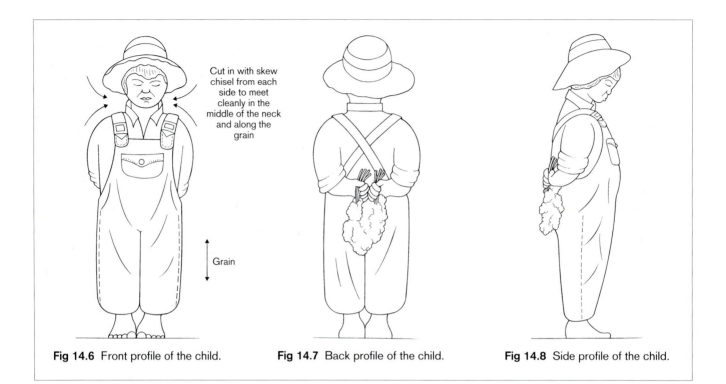

Cut in with skew
chisel from each
side to meet
cleanly in the
middle of the neck
and along the
grain

Grain

Fig 14.6 Front profile of the child.

Fig 14.7 Back profile of the child.

Fig 14.8 Side profile of the child.

Roughing
out the child

As with the standing man project in Chapter
10, draw the front, back, side and top
profiles of the child (Figs 14.6, 14.7, 14.8 and
14.9) on the wood and, if you do not have a
bandsaw, make saw cuts from the edges to
the projections and indents of the figure,
allowing the waste to be removed with the
1in (25mm) no. 3 gouge. Then round off the
square corners of the figure with the ¼in
(6mm) no. 5 or no. 6 gouge and smooth
them, removing any remaining saw cuts,
with the ½ and ¼in (13 and 6mm) no. 3
gouges.

Bear in mind that, initially, any clothed
figure should be made oversize to allow for
the depth of the creases and folds of the

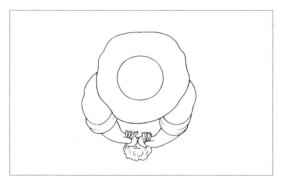

Fig 14.9 Overhead view of the child.

material. These are curved into the surface
of the figure to reflect the shape of the body
underneath the clothing.

Working from the sides of the figure, use
the ¼in (6mm) no. 5 or no. 6 gouge to round
over the shoulders towards the neck, and
shape the edge of the hat brim to fit around
the head. Remove the ridges left by the tool
with the ½ and ¼in (13 and 6mm) no. 3
gouges (see Fig 14.10). By scooping upwards

Fig 14.10 Round over the shoulders and shape the edge of the hat brim.

Fig 14.11 Round the sides and chest.

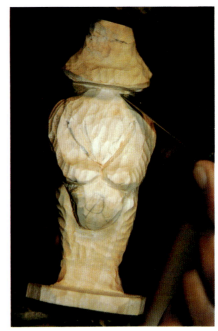

Fig 14.12 Work from beneath the hat brim to lower the shoulders.

and *with* the grain, reduce and round the circumference of the hat crown so that the brim projects all around it. Beneath the brim, round off the square corners remaining from the saw cuts using the ¼in (6mm) no. 5 or no. 6 gouge (see Fig 14.9), leaving the brim and head as one: if you undercut it at this stage, it may become broken as you work. Round the backs of the shoulders and arms, working up towards the back of the neck, followed by rounding the sides and chest towards the front of the neck (see Fig 14.11).

Next, draw the outlines of the arms and hands, which hold a bunch of kale behind the child's back. The kale should be left as a block for now, to be carved in detail later. Using the opposing-cut method with the ½ or ¼in (13 or 6mm) no. 3 gouges, form channels along the inner and outer edges of each arm, and remove the adjacent wood to leave the arms standing proud of the torso so that they can be rounded. Around the kale, remove the excess wood using the ¼in (6mm) no. 5 or no. 6 gouge to the depth of the seat and tops of the thighs, then, with the same tool, round the remaining squared corners of the legs. Finally, deepen the small of the back, hollow the surface of the arm slightly, round off the kale, and smooth the surfaces with the ½ and ¼in (13 and 6mm) no. 3 gouges.

Round the toes with the ¼in (6mm) no. 5 or no. 6 gouge. Using the ¼ and ⅛in (6 or 3mm) no. 3 gouges, shape the feet, blending the ends of the trousers into the tops of the feet, and then scrape the surfaces smooth.

Working from beneath the back of the hat brim, lower the shoulders (as shown in Fig 14.12). Then re-cut the edge of the brim and the sides of the head until the face is fully rounded at the front. Form the neck with the skew chisel, twisting it sideways to cut down, then up, so that you work with the grain to create a clean hollow on each side of the neck. Reduce the surface of the chest below the chin and carve a gentle hollow to run around and link the sides of the neck. Since this involves cutting across the grain, use a narrow, deeply curved tool, such as a ⅛in (3mm) no. 10 gouge, to form the hollow. Slightly undercut the jaw line with the ¼in (6mm) no. 3 gouge, and round its edge gently into the hollow. Now extend the neck by removing more of the chest surface, and reduce its circumference.

Shape and position the crown of the hat, using first the ¼in (6mm) no. 5 gouge and then the ¼in (6mm) no. 3, so that it corresponds with the head, but leave undercutting the brim and shaping the upper part of the head until later. Pare the entire figure smooth by hand, using the no. 3 gouges, then scrape it so that it is ready for the more intricate detail work.

Carving the detail

Intricate detail work, which adds a great deal of interest to a figure, can be regarded as relief carving, since the same channelling and paring techniques are employed. However, it is essential that the surfaces to be detailed are perfectly smooth, otherwise it is impossible to make clean cuts and obtain tidy results. Make sure your tools are razor sharp before you begin, and be ready to re-sharpen them if required while you are working.

The clothing

Draw the dungarees, shirt collar and rolled up sleeves on the figure in pencil. Next, use the ⅛in (3mm) V tool to cut a channel around the open collar at the neck, or use the opposing-cut method with the ¼ or ⅛in (6 or 3mm) no. 3 gouge. Since access is restricted, form the neck within the collar by paring its surface towards the collar, slicing sideways with the skew chisel. Cut channels around the wings of the collar, to the back of the neck, and make the collar stand proud by reducing the adjacent surface of the shirt.

Outline the straps and bib of the dungarees with V-channels (as shown in Fig 14.13), and reduce the surface of the shirt so that they stand proud. Continue the straps of the dungarees over the shoulders, making them appear to cross at the back of the figure by reducing the lower strap on each side of the

Fig 14.13 Outline the straps and bib with V-channels.

upper strap. Again, reduce the surface of the shirt to make them stand proud (see Fig 14.14).

The pockets should be made to stand proud in the same manner as those of the standing man carved in Chapter 10 (see page 131), and then a channel cut between the legs, at both back and front, working along the grain with the ⅛in (3mm) V tool. Shape each leg by slicing sideways into the channel with the ¼in (6mm) no. 3 gouge, held bevel uppermost. Mark the ends of the trousers with V-channels, using either the V tool or the no. 3 gouge, and shape the ankles beneath them by paring up towards each channel. At this stage, you will probably find that the base of the figure is beginning to obstruct your cuts, so reduce its circumference by carefully using the ½in (13mm) no. 3 gouge to slice slivers from the edge and re-chamfer it.

Fig 14.14 At the back, make the straps appear to cross by reducing the lower strap where it meets the upper strap.

Cut channels around the top and bottom of the rolled up portion of each sleeve, reducing the surface of the sleeve above and arm below. Then shape and scrape the rolled portions in preparation for carving the folds later.

The feet

Ideally, when you carve the feet, refer to a good anatomy book and study your own feet, or those of a child, so that your work will be accurate. Remember that a child's foot is plump and rounded and, with the exception of the big toe, the toes curl downwards.

Draw the outline of the toes on the top of each foot and, since you will be working in end grain, use the ⅛in (3mm) V tool to separate them. Then pare the surface of each foot with a ¼ or ⅛in (6 or 3mm) no. 3 gouge so that it flows smoothly into the ankle. Shape the heels and toes with the ¹⁄₁₆in (2mm) no. 5 and ¼in (6mm) no. 3 gouges, and the point of the skew chisel, removing minute parings until you achieve the correct shape. Then scrape the surfaces using the ends of the no. 3 gouges and the skew chisel.

The hands

Both hands are crooked, grasping the stalks of the kale, and they are complicated to carve. You may find it useful to duplicate each arm and hand in Plasticine first, and keep them nearby so that you can compare them with your carving (see Fig 14.15). Initially, treat each hand as a mitten, carving the separate fingers later.

The ends of the kale stalks need to project above each hand, as does the inner edge of the

Fig 14.15 (above left) Modelling the hands in Plasticine may help in carving them correctly.

Fig 14.16 (above right) Cut creases and folds in the dungarees, shaping them around the figure.

gripping thumb. Use the opposing-cut method and the ⅛ or ¹⁄₁₆in (3 or 2mm) no. 3 gouge to cut channels outlining the stalks, then reduce the surface of the hand beneath them so that they stand proud. Next, cut around the end of the thumb and reduce the surface of the hand beneath it so that it appears to be wrapped around the stalks. Use the ¹⁄₁₆in (2mm) no. 5 gouge to shape the heel of the hand until it flows smoothly into the wrist and forearm.

Cut another channel from the end of the thumb to outline the forefinger, the tips of the remaining fingers and the heel of the hand, allowing the hand to be shaped. Angle this at the knuckle joints so that it appears to be gripping the stalks. Scrape the surface, leaving the fingers to be marked later.

Remove the surface of the kale below

each hand, using the ¼ or ⅛in (6 or 3mm) no. 3 gouge, until it is in line with the stalks emerging above the hand. Then smooth the surface and draw on the lobes of the kale so that they are hanging downwards. Using the ¹⁄₁₆in (2mm) no. 3 and no. 5 gouges, cut channels around the lobes and shape them so that they appear to overlap each other, leaving the edges to be undercut later.

Form the fingers by lightly incising the ¹⁄₁₆in (2mm) no. 3 gouge into the wood to cut channels between them. Then pare the sides of the fingers over into the channels. Finally, texture the stalks emerging from the hands with the small hook that projects from the junction of the blades of the ⅛in (3mm) V tool, working upwards *with* the grain.

The face and hat

If access to the head is difficult, reduce the size of the hat brim, but still refrain from undercutting it, as it will be vulnerable to accidental damage. Before you attempt to carve the face, the head must be symmetrical and smooth, and the neck and jaw line must be established.

Hollow the eye sockets with the ¹⁄₁₆in (2mm) no. 3 and no. 5 gouges, reducing the cheeks and the area beneath the nose to leave the nose proud. Next, reduce the chin, leaving the mouth slightly raised. Pare both mouth and nose to tiny triangular mounds, blending the edges smoothly into the surrounding surfaces. Invert the no. 5 gouge to cut the curved lids of the downcast eyes, then use the point of the skew chisel to round the eyes and scrape them smooth. Cut the hairline around the face, and shape the top of the head inside the crown of the hat with the ¼ or ⅛in (6 or 3mm) no. 3 gouge, texturing the hair by carving narrow channels with the hook on the ⅛in (3mm) V tool.

Reshape the hat crown with the ⅛in (3mm) no. 10 gouge so that it matches the head below, and saw off the top at an angle with a hacksaw. Adjust the size and shape of the brim as necessary, and smooth the hat by paring with the ¼in (6mm) no. 3 gouge. Scrape it smooth.

Make opposing cuts with the ¼in (6mm) no. 3 gouge or the ⅛in (3mm) V tool to mark the edges of the hatband, and pare the adjacent surface to leave it slightly raised. The straw texturing of the hat is achieved by indenting the surface in a regular pattern. I used a light hammer and a small rectangular punch filed with a series of teeth for this, but any piece of metal could have points filed on it, or you could bind several stout pins or fine nails together with masking tape and tap these into the surface instead.

Finishing the clothing

Each of the dungaree straps should have a buckle, carved as a simple open rectangle, with the end of the strap emerging from beneath it, while the pocket flap on the bib needs a central button. These should be carved with the ⅛ and ¹⁄₁₆in (3 and 2mm) no. 3 gouges. Cut the folds around the rolled up shirt sleeves with the ¼ and ⅛in (6 and 3mm) no. 3 gouges, tidying the areas where the arms, sleeves and chest meet with the point of the skew chisel.

Using the ⅛in (3mm) no. 10 gouge, cut several curved creases or folds on the dungarees, shaping them gently around the figure (as shown in Fig 14.16). Do not overdo these, as they will look contrived. The stitching on the seams of the dungarees can be marked with the punch used for texturing the hat, tilting the tool and pressing its edge into the wood by hand. Alternatively, pierce the lines of stitching with the point of the skew chisel, or of a nail. At this point, the lobes of the kale foliage can be undercut with the ⅛in (3mm) no. 3 gouge.

Re-cut the ends of the trousers to fit around the ankles, then undercut the ends by scooping with the ⅛in (3mm) no. 10 gouge, extending and reshaping the ankles within the trouser legs. Finally, undercut the brim of the hat, but only close to the head so that you leave plenty of thickness at the edge for strength.

Finishing

Since a child's skin is smooth, scrape the arms, feet and face, then abrade only the skin surfaces with 320 grit garnet paper, to remove any tool marks. Examine the angles between all adjoining surfaces to ensure that they are cleanly cut. Smooth the base and round its edges with the ¼ or ½in (6 or 13mm) no. 3 gouge. Apply Danish oil to all the figures with a small brush, followed by a good quality wax polish when it has dried.

I arranged the sheep and child on a base made from a slice of elm, but any wood or bark with a contrasting colour would have been suitable. The figures can be mounted permanently by gluing them to the base, inserting dowels between them for added strength, or temporarily with small, hidden pieces of Blu-Tak adhesive, which is available from stationery shops.

Chapter 15
Detailed Figure Carving
'Mrs Daley'

Several years ago, I carved the original 'Mrs Daley' from a log of yew, using the sapwood so that she had a lighter coloured bandana around her head. Since then, she has proved so popular with the visitors at shows where I demonstrate carving, that her ample rear is building up a nice patina from all the casual stroking!

'Mrs Daley' is an ideal subject for a landscaped carving, that is one where the central figure and all its accessories are carved from the same piece of wood. However, you need not copy her exactly, since the carving could easily be altered to depict, for example, a workman, such as a carpenter or plumber, kneeling at an appropriate task.

Unlike the previous figure projects, in Chapters 10 and 14, where the subjects were symmetrically posed so that the front, back and side profiles could be cut initially with a bandsaw or saw and gouge, this one is carved directly into the wood. Although a more advanced approach, it is a very enjoyable way of working that can be used freely for any subject once you have mastered the basic carving techniques, which you will have done if you have worked through the projects in the previous chapters.

Tools you will need

- ½in (13mm) no. 9 gouge
- ¼in (6mm) no. 9 gouge
- ¼in (6mm) no. 5 gouge
- ½in (13mm) no. 3 (Swiss no. 2) gouge
- ¼in (6mm) no. 3 (Swiss no. 2) gouge
- ³⁄₁₆in (5mm) no. 3 (Swiss no. 2) gouge
- ⅛in (3mm) no. 3 (Swiss no. 2) gouge
- ¹⁄₁₆in (2mm) no. 3 (Swiss no. 2) gouge
- ⅛in (3mm) no. 8, no. 9 or no. 10 gouge
- ¼in (6mm) skew chisel

- ⅛ or ¼in (3 or 6mm) 60° V tool
- ¼in (6mm) no. 5 (Swiss no. 25) back-bent gouge
- ¼in (6mm) no. 5 (Swiss cut 7a) front-bent gouge
- Mallet
- Nail and light hammer
- Cabinet scraper
- Saw
- Hand drill and ¼in (6mm) wood bit (optional)

Choosing and preparing the wood

I used a block of lime, measuring 9½in (238mm) long by 6in (150mm) wide and 4in (100mm) deep, with the grain running lengthwise. Lime was chosen because it shows detail well in photographs, but normally I would have used a wood with a more interesting grain pattern, such as yew, walnut, plum or cherry, to enhance the finished carving. In fact, any of the fine-grained woods listed in the glossary on page 175 would have been suitable, provided it was sound and well seasoned.

You could use a log instead of a block, preparing it in the same manner as the hedgehog in Chapter 6 by removing the bark and cambium layer below with a large no. 3 gouge and mallet until you reach sound wood.

Choose one side of the log as the base, making sure that the shape is as symmetrical as possible when viewed from the ends, then saw and flatten the surface with a plane or Surform until the log stands steadily without rocking. If the log is a large one, slicing off a section by sawing along the grain with a ripsaw can be tiring. In this case, you may find it easier to make a series of cuts across the grain and remove the waste wood between them with your widest chisel or no. 3 gouge and mallet, as you did when removing the waste from the figures in Chapters 10 and 14.

Starting the figure

Draw a horizontal line around the block, about ¾in (19mm) from the bottom edge to indicate the top edge of the floor. Then draw a second horizontal line about ¼in (6mm) above this to

Fig 15.1 (above) Side views of figure.

Fig 15.2 (right) Front, back and top views of figure.

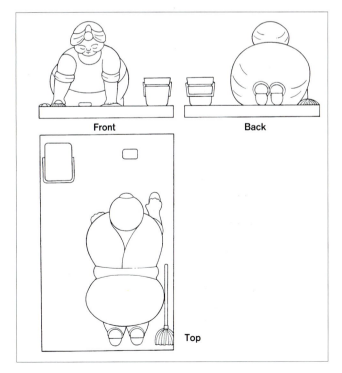

Front

Back

Top

161

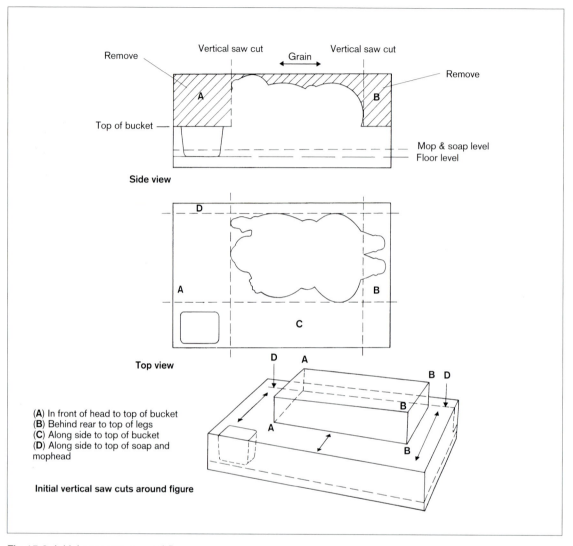

Side view

Top view

(A) In front of head to top of bucket
(B) Behind rear to top of legs
(C) Along side to top of bucket
(D) Along side to top of soap and mophead

Initial vertical saw cuts around figure

Remove

Vertical saw cut

Grain

Vertical saw cut

Remove

A

B

Top of bucket

Mop & soap level
Floor level

D

A

B

C

D

A

B D

B

A

B

Fig 15.3 Initial saw cuts around figure.

indicate the tops of the mop and soap, which will be carved in relief from the base at a later stage. Then draw the top and side views of the figure, and the bucket, on to the wood (see Figs 15.1 and 15.2).

Refer to Fig 15.3 and make the vertical saw cut **A**, from in front of the head down to the level of the bucket top. Remove the waste wood to the bottom of this cut by chipping along the grain with the 1in (25mm) no. 3 gouge. Repeat this process at the rear of the

figure, making the vertical saw cut **B** behind the rump, down to the level of the tops of the heels. Draw the top views of the bucket and the legs on the freshly cut surfaces.

Next, make the vertical saw cuts **C** and **D**, shown in Fig 15.3, along each side of the figure down to the level of the bucket top. Using the 1in (25mm) no. 3 gouge, chip along the grain to remove the waste wood on the left-hand (bucket) side of the figure only, carefully splitting off narrow slivers of wood. Then

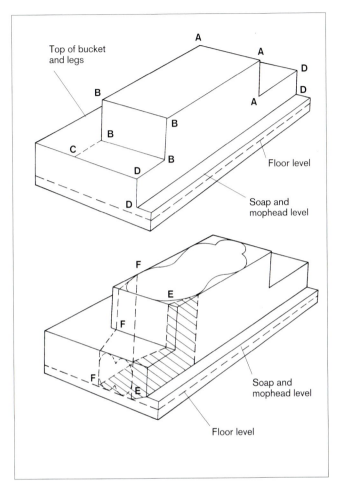

Fig 15.4 Second set of saw cuts.

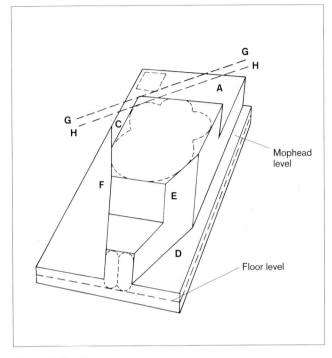

Fig 15.5 Final saw cuts.

continue the saw cut **D** down to the line indicating the tops of the soap and mop head. Remove the waste wood on this side of figure in the same manner as on the left, using the no. 3 gouge (see Fig 15.4).

Still referring to Fig 15.4, make the vertical saw cuts **E** and **F** along each side of the legs, down to the mop head and soap line. Again, remove the waste wood with the no. 3 gouge. Now make the vertical saw cuts **G** and **H** (shown in Fig 15.5) between the bucket and head, down to the mop head and soap line, allowing for the outstretched arm. Remove excess wood from these areas: alongside the figure, **F** and **C** to saw cut **G**, leaving the bucket as a block; the triangular area between the head and bucket that falls between saw cuts **G** and **H**, down to the level of the top of the bucket; area **A** beside the bucket and in front of the figure.

Finally, make the bucket a rectangular block by sawing down to the level of the mop head and soap, cutting off the waste (see Fig 15.5). Gently round off the corners of the base before beginning to shape the figure.

Beginning the shaping

Because the grain of the wood will run across the arms, both hands of the figure need to be in contact with the floor, otherwise the arms could easily break off. To add interest, the

Fig 15.6 (below) Round over the rump and sides of figure.

Fig 15.7 (right) Round the top of the head, shoulders and arms, making the right arm extend forwards and down.

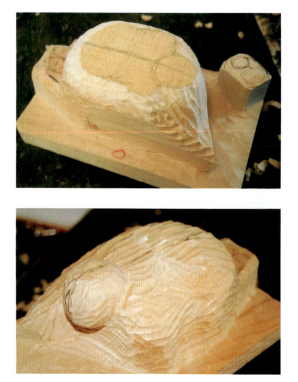

Fig 15.8 Round the front of the figure so that the head begins to protrude.

right arm is reaching ahead, while the hand holds a scrubbing brush with its bristles touching the floor. The palm of the left hand is clutching a duster and almost flat on the floor, so the figure is well supported.

Draw a centre-line along the length of the figure and round off the rump in the same manner as the hedgehog in Chapter 6, using the ½in (13mm) no. 9 gouge. Round over the tops and the sides of the legs (as shown in Fig 15.6). This area needs to be well rounded. At the front of the figure, round the sides of the arms, the shoulders and the top of the head, making the right arm slope forwards to the base (as shown in Fig 15.7). Then round the corners of the bucket with the ½in (13mm) no. 3 gouge to provide better access to the figure.

Scoop a hollow in the end grain at the front of the shoulders and along each side of the head, cutting outwards and across the grain with the ½in (13mm), then ¼in (6mm) no. 9 gouges. Next, round over the shoulders and sides of the body, extending the hollows at the sides of the head to meet under the chin (see Fig 15.8), so that the head begins to protrude in front of the shoulders and chest, and along the inside of the extended right arm with the same tool. Lower each shoulder and round the front of the head into a ball-like shape. When doing this, you will not be able to avoid cutting against the grain, but if your tools are really sharp, any tearing of the wood will be minimal.

Using the opposing-cut method with the ¼in (6mm) no. 3 gouge, continue the hollows at

Fig 15.9 Shape the head into a ball.

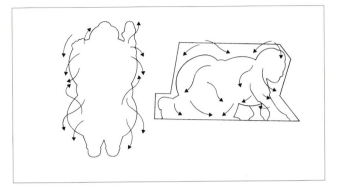

Fig 15.10 Shape the figure by cutting curved paths over and around it.

each side of the head by cutting curved channels that meet at the back of the head. Then reduce the area of the back below the head. Repeat this several times until the head is raised above the back, at which point it can be rounded over into the channel and shaped into a ball (as shown in Fig 15.9), using the ½in (13mm) no. 3 gouge, bevel uppermost, to smooth it.

Working from the sides of the figure, round the corners of the hips and upper body with the ¼in (6mm) no. 9 gouge. Then begin forming the hollow on each side of the waist by cutting towards the waist from both the back of the shoulders and the hips, continuing down to the base in preparation for drilling through later.

Narrow the shoulders, using the ¼in (6mm) no. 9 gouge, so that the rump is the widest part of the figure. If necessary, reduce the size of the head accordingly.

Next, work over the entire figure so that it is completely rounded and feels comfortable when handled. This process takes time, but is essential if the figure is to have a tactile quality. Generally speaking, if a carving feels right in your hands, it will look right.

Whenever the centre-line is removed, re-draw it immediately so that you have a fixed point of reference, allowing you to compare the shape of each side of the figure and adjust it so that it is anatomically symmetrical. Narrow and taper the legs by removing wood from the outer side of each. Then tidy the angles between adjacent surfaces, making sure they are cleanly cut and paying particular attention to the area behind the head. Use the V tool to clean the angle between the figure and the base.

You can see from the photographs how the gouge is guided around the shape with long, sweeping cuts so that the planes of the figure merge, rather than remaining as separate flat areas. This is achieved by cutting curved paths over and across the figure (as shown in Fig 15.10), yet *with* the grain. If you can master this way of working, and provided you have a clear picture in your mind of what you are carving, you can use all manner of pieces of wood without being restricted to the 'squared block, drawing profiles and rounding the corners' method, which often makes it difficult to remove the 'squareness' from the piece. As with all carving, it will be helpful to hold the work in your hands and cover areas with your thumbs and fingers to see where wood should

Fig 15.11 (left) Smooth the figure by paring with a no. 3 gouge held bevel uppermost.

Fig 15.12 (below) Round the legs and draw on the soles of the shoes.

be removed. Shade unwanted areas with pencil and pare them away.

Finally, remove the marks left by the no. 9 gouge by paring with the 1in (25mm) no. 3 gouge, held bevel uppermost. Guide this over and around the figure until it is smooth and rounded, with no gouge grooves remaining (see Fig 15.11).

Carving the legs

The heels form the highest points of the outstretched legs, which slope down towards the bent knees and the edge of the skirt. Make a shallow saw cut across the back of the knees, cutting in towards the thighs, then use the 1in (25mm) no. 3 gouge to form a gentle slope along the calves towards the rump, rounding over the outer edges of the thighs. Next, mark

the inner edge of each leg with the V tool, and cut a hollow between them with the ¼in (6mm) no. 9 gouge, ready for drilling later. Round the inner edge of each leg with the ½in (13mm) no. 3 gouge tilted sideways to pare along the grain on each side. Draw the soles of the feet in line with the legs (see Fig 15.12), and round the outer edges of the legs on to the base, following the outlines of the soles with the ¼in (6mm) no. 9 gouge. Narrow the ankles and heels, and round the length of each leg so that it tapers towards the heel, using the same tool, followed by the ¼in (6mm) no. 3 gouge to smooth them.

Draw in the side views of the legs, ankles, heels and feet, then use the ¼in (6mm) no. 3 gouge to cut a hollow beneath the shins, ankles and top of each foot. Smooth the adjacent area of the base, ready for drilling beneath the feet.

Carving between the arms

Draw the outline of the arms and bosom on the chest, then scoop a hollow between the arms and under the bosom, using the ¼in (6mm) no. 9 gouge. Continue cutting until it is no longer possible to work outwards with the grain. Remove the outer surface of the left arm to narrow it by cutting around it with the ¼in (6mm) no. 9 gouge. Follow a spiral path as you cut to reduce the size of the arm, but

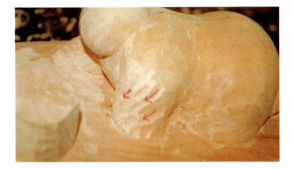

Fig 15.13 Reduce the size of the left arm by making spiral cuts down its length.

Fig 15.14 From each side, bore a hole through under the shins, with another to meet it between the ankles. Use a similar technique to open up the area between the arms and beneath the bosom and waist.

retain its shape (marked in red in Fig 15.13). Smooth the base between the arms, ready for drilling beneath the bosom towards the knees. Round over the inner and outer edges of the outstretched right arm by slicing outwards and upwards along its length with a ½in (13mm) no. 3 gouge.

Drilling

Although it is possible to carve through from each side, drilling saves time and effort, as long as it is carried out carefully and accurately. When drilling through a carving, it is better to carve an initial hollow on each side and drill halfway through from each hollow, as this removes the possibility of the drill bit 'breaking out' through the side of the carving and splintering it, or damaging the carving because the hole was drilled at the wrong angle.

Use the ¼in (6mm) drill bit and hand drill to bore the following holes in the carving: horizontally between the shin and upper foot from each side (see Fig 15.14); vertically between the legs to meet the previous hole, wrapping adhesive tape around the bit to act as a depth guide; horizontally under the waist from each side (two or three, as necessary); two

horizontally from the front, beneath the bosom, keeping well inside the arms to meet the hole under the waist, again using tape as a depth guide. Enlarge each hole and open up the gaps beneath the figure, using the ¼in (6mm) no. 3, no. 5 and no. 9 gouges under the waist, and the ³⁄₁₆in (5mm) no. 3 gouge and ¼in (6mm) skew chisel between the legs. Smooth the base inside each opening so that it blends in with the surface around the outside of the figure.

Refining the legs and feet

As a rule, it is best to carve and finish the less accessible inner surfaces and edges first, so that they will not need any further attention. The outer and more accessible surfaces can then be finished, so that the carving is complete. Don't do this the other way round, as the outer surfaces will suffer damage when you finish the inner ones.

Reduce the size of the heels with the ¼ or ⅛in (6 or 3mm) no. 3 gouge then channel the outline of each shoe heel with the ¼in (6mm)

Fig 15.15 Shape the legs and ankles into the shoes, then adjust the rump to keep it in proportion.

no. 3 gouge, paring the surface of the ankle to fit within the shoe. Since access between the ankles will be restricted, use the ¼in (6mm) no. 5 back-bent gouge to blend each inner ankle into the top of the foot, and to clean up the base and edges of the legs where they meet the base. Continue the channel that marks the edge of the shoe underneath each foot, then shape the outer surface of the leg and ankle into the top of the shoe. Adjust each side of the rump as necessary to bring it back into proportion with the legs (see Fig 15.15).

Clearing between the arms and under the bosom

Carefully split small slivers of wood away along the edges of the drilled holes, towards the space in front of the waist, enlarging the

gap between the arms. Continue until there is enough space to use the ¼in (6mm) no. 5 back-bent gouge to round the back of each arm and merge the bosom into the waist. As you work, periodically re-cut the edges of the arms and knees where they meet the base, using the V tool. Smooth all surfaces with no. 3 gouges and the skew chisel, twisting the latter to cut sideways, thus *with* the grain.

Starting the soap and mop

Draw the soap and mop on the base, cut around them with the V tool, and carve them in relief, using the ½ and ¼in (13 and 6mm) no. 3 gouges to deepen the channels. Next, using the same tools, lower the entire surface of the base, around and beneath the figure, to the level of the line drawn around the block. In the process, extend the arms and leave the mop head, its handle and the soap to be detailed later.

Preparing the carving for detailing

As mentioned in previous chapters, detailing can be regarded as relief carving, but before you start, make sure that the surfaces to be detailed are smooth, correctly shaped and in proportion, also that your tools are razor sharp. Be prepared to spend plenty of time on preparing the carving for detailing, going over the entire figure again and again until it is perfect. Do not be tempted to carve fine details too soon, as you may end up removing them as you alter parts of the figure to keep them in proportion. Use the 1in (25mm) no. 3 gouge, bevel uppermost, to smooth and round the rump with a sliding, slicing action, until no flat surfaces remain. Make sure the angles between all adjacent surfaces are cleanly cut and tidy, and smooth the bosom/waist area beneath the figure.

The arms, hands and scrubbing brush

Reduce the circumference of each arm so that it tapers towards the forearm, and separate the chest from the inner arms to form the armpits with the skew chisel, twisting its blade sideways and cutting forwards with the grain.

Using the opposing-cut method with the ¼in (6mm) no. 3 gouge, mark the line of the back of each arm against the torso, then round each side and the bosom underneath into the waist of the figure. Working from each side, use the two bent gouges by hand to shape the waist and bosom symmetrically along each side from the armpits. Then round the edges of the arms along their length with the ½ or ¼in (13 or 6mm) no. 3 gouge. Mark the outline of the left hand with the V tool, and pare the wrist into the top of the hand resting on the floor (see Fig 15.16). Smooth this area, ready for the fingers and duster to be detailed later.

Next, establish the top of the scrubbing brush, using the ¼in (6mm) no. 3 gouge to shape it into a rectangular block beneath the hand/arm (see Fig 15.17). Leave sufficient width so that the outline of the hand, initially as a mitten lying over the side of the brush, can be marked with the V tool. Then use the ⅛in (3mm)

Fig 15.16 Outline the left hand with the V tool, and shape the hand into the wrist.

Fig 15.17 Shape the right arm to leave a rectangular block for the scrubbing brush.

Fig 15.18 Carve the right hand in relief, leaving it as a mitten shape at this stage.

no 3 gouge to cut the hand in relief, leaving it proud of the brush and smoothed, ready for carving the fingers in due course (see Fig 15.18).

Use the V tool and a ¼in (6mm) no. 3 gouge with opposing cuts to pare the wrists and carve the thumb in relief so that it is wrapped over the inner edge of the brush and linked to the edge of the palm and top of the hand. To obtain the correct shape in this area, you may find it helpful to refer to an anatomy book or study your own hand gripping a similar object. Creating the shape in Plasticine, as when carving the hands of the child in Chapter 14, is another useful exercise.

The clothing and shoes

Draw the rolled portions of the sleeves around the arms, and outline them with the V tool. Pare the surface of the forearms below them with the ¼in (6mm) no. 3 gouge to leave the sleeves proud of the arms. Then reshape the wrists, forearms and hands so that they are in proportion again, leaving the detail of the fingers until later. Use the V tool to mark the edges of the armholes in the overall, and reduce the surface of the sleeves below these so that the overall stands slightly proud (see Fig 15.19).

Now shape the sides of the thighs, working under towards the waist and bosom, and around to the front of the thighs. This area should be blended into a fold where the bosom meets the waist, being smoothed with the ½in (13mm) no. 3 gouge, held bevel uppermost and used with a slicing action *across* the grain until all the surfaces are smooth and cleanly cut. Finally, outline the waistband with the V tool, and pare back the surface on each side to leave it standing proud with the ¼in (6mm) no. 3 gouge.

Re-adjust the shape of the rump as necessary, then cut a gentle hollow along the edge of the skirt to correspond with the shape of the backs of the legs emerging from beneath

it, using the ¼in (6mm) no. 9 gouge. Smooth the hollow with the skew chisel, twisting its blade to cut outwards *with* the grain. Do not undercut the edge of the skirt at this stage. Once again, shape the legs into the tops of the shoes, paring with the ½in (13mm) no. 3 gouge to narrow the ankles and heels as necessary.

Mark the line of the heel in the end grain across the sole of each shoe with the V tool and use the ¼ or ⅛in (6 or 3mm) no. 3 gouge to scoop back the sole beneath it to form the instep (see Fig 15.20). To add interest, use the same gouge to curl the toes of the left foot underneath by undercutting the upper surface of the foot from beneath the shin, then hollow the instep of the other foot to stretch the foot out backwards. Finally, mark the edge of the sole around each shoe and reduce the adjacent surface of the uppers slightly.

Outline the cross-over of the overall straps

Fig 15.19 Outlining the armholes of the overall with the V tool.

Fig 15.20 Cut back the soles of the shoes towards the instep.

on the chest with the V tool, and reduce the surface of the blouse in the same manner as the sleeves. Then set the neck within the collar of the blouse, deepening the base of the neck and hollowing further under the chin as necessary with the ¼in (6mm) no. 5 or no. 3 gouge. You are now ready to begin carving the face.

Carving the head and face

Since the face is in end grain, carving fine detail will not be easy, as the fibres will tend to break and pull out. Your tools must be razor sharp, as inevitably you will have to work against the grain at some point. Make sure that the head is smooth and symmetrical before beginning.

Mark the outline of the bandana with the V tool, and pare away the surface of the head below it, making sure the head remains rounded and smooth by adjusting the shape with the ½in (13mm) no. 3 gouge, held bevel uppermost. Hollow the eye sockets with a ⅛in (3mm) no. 8, no. 9 or no. 10 gouge, reducing the surface beneath the nose to leave it proud. Using the ⅛ and ¹⁄₁₆in (3 and 2mm) no. 3 gouges, make tiny paring cuts to hollow both nasolabial furrows, round each cheek to the sides of the head, and create hollows down each side of the mouth to the mound of the chin and under the jaw. Outline the earlobes that peep from beneath the edge of the bandanna, reduce the sides and back of the neck in proportion, then smooth the top and back of the head, ready for detailing the bandana.

Outline the knot and ends of the bandana with the V tool, then carve it in relief with the small no. 3 gouges (see Fig 15.21). At the same

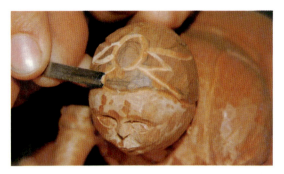

Fig 15.21 Carve the knot and ends of the bandana in relief, using small no. 3 gouges.

time, adjust the height of the bandana so that it appears to fit over the head, rather than being perched on top. If you wish, add extra interest by carving earrings in very shallow relief on the cheeks, so that they appear to dangle from the earlobes beneath the bandanna, and mark strands of hair using the hook of the V tool.

Finishing the edges of the skirt

Using the V tool, mark the edge of the skirt across the backs of the legs and around each side of the figure, then undercut this by scooping outwards from below with the ¼in (6mm) no. 3 gouge. Where the legs meet the edge of the skirt, pare the surface smooth to remove any remaining deep cuts or nicks.

Detailing the mop

Narrow and round the handle of the mop by paring with the ¼in (6mm) no. 3 gouge, then round the head into the handle. Carve the mop head into an uneven shape, smooth it and cut the edges cleanly, smoothing the adjacent floor surface with the same gouge. Finally, mark the

Fig 15.22 Undercut the edges of the mop to make the handle appear rounded.

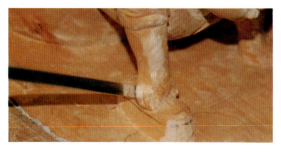

Fig 15.23 Carve the fingers of the right hand, then shape the back of the hand into the wrist.

strands of the head with the ⅛in (3mm) V tool, and undercut each side of the handle until it appears round in cross-section (see Fig 15.22).

Finishing the hands and brush

Using a V tool to mark the tiny fingers might tear the surface of the wood, so instead employ the opposing-cut method with the ⅛ and ¹⁄₁₆in (3 and 2mm) no. 3 gouges to cut channels, as you did when carving the child's hands in Chapter 14. For the right hand, outline the edge of the forefinger, across the top of the brush, continuing the channel to mark the inside of the thumb lying over the edge of the brush. Round over both finger and thumb, reducing the adjacent surface of the brush. Next, divide the mitten-shaped hand into four fingers, cutting channels between them and rounding them over to resemble sausages. Shorten the third and little fingers, leaving the middle finger as the longest, then shape the back of the hand into the wrist (see Fig 15.23).

The V tool can be used to outline the brush handle, but take care not to cut through the thumb and forefinger gripping each side. Form the bristles by paring towards the V-channel

with the skew chisel or ⅛in (3mm) no. 3 gouge to create an overhang, and reduce the surface of the handle on each side of the thumb and forefinger. Smooth the surface of the bristles, then make vertical cuts by hand using the hook of the V tool to mark them. Finally, using the ¼ and ⅛in (6 and 3mm) gouges, undercut the ends of the bristles slightly, and remove any nicks left by the V tool in the adjacent surface.

For the left hand, cut the curve from forefinger to thumb with the ⅛in (3mm) no. 3 gouge, and reduce the surface of the duster beneath. Cut each finger as for the right hand, marking a ring around the third finger, and shape the back of the hand into the wrist. Outline the duster on the floor with the V tool, and carve it in relief with the ¼ and ⅛in (6 or 3mm) no. 3 gouges (see Fig 15.24). Form the edges of the duster and tidy the adjacent surfaces with the ¼ and ½in (6 and 13mm) no. 3 gouges, together with the skew chisel.

Detailing the bucket

Round the corners of the bucket slightly, and undercut its base a little. Using the V tool, outline the handle, then pare back the adjacent

Fig 15.24 Carve the duster beneath the left hand in relief.

Fig 15.25 Tap the point of a nail into the wood to simulate perforations in the mop bucket.

Fig 15.26 Outline the puddle of water with the V tool, then carve gentle curves in it to simulate ripples.

surface with the ¼ and ⅛in (6 or 3mm) no. 3 gouges to leave the handle proud. Reshape the corners of the bucket and round over the handle.

A mop bucket has two divisions: one is used for 'parking' the mop when not in use, for which there is an indentation in the division; the other is like a perforated bowl in which the water is squeezed from the mop head. Outline the two sections with the V tool and hollow each. To suggest the perforations in the bowl section, make a regular pattern of indentations by gently tapping the point of a nail into the surface with a light hammer (see Fig 15.25). The same technique can be used to form the rivets of the bucket, and the soap suds in the other section.

The soap and water

Gently round the corners of the tablet of soap, and undercut its edges slightly where it meets the floor to make it look used. Then smooth the surrounding floor surface with the ¼ and ½in (3 and 6mm) no. 3 gouges and the skew chisel.

A puddle of water around the scrubbing brush makes a nice touch. Draw its shape on the wood and outline it with the V tool, reducing the adjacent floor area with the no. 3 gouges and skew chisel. To make the surface of the water look rippled, cut gentle curving hollows with a ⅛in (3mm) no. 8, no. 9 or no. 10 gouge (see Fig 15.26). To suggest clusters of foam and soap bubbles, tap the point of the nail gently into the surface.

Detailing the shoe soles and stockings

Use the hammer and nail again to create the tread on the soles of the shoes. Then use the V tool to cut around the ankles, forming the wrinkles and folds in the stockings. Round over the edges of the cuts of soften them. Finally, use the point of the nail to mark a wavering line along the back of each leg to suggest the stocking seams (see Fig 15.27).

Detailing the clothing

Mark the stitching around the armholes of the overall with the point of the nail, then cut several tiny creases that emanate from beneath the waistband, and add a button for the fastener, carving this in relief with the ⅟₁₆in (2mm) no. 3 gouge (see Fig 15.28). Next, carve several curving folds in the skirt material across the knees, using a ⅛in (3mm) no. 8, no. 9 or no. 10 gouge. Soften the edges of the cuts with the ¼ and ⅛in (6 and 3mm) no. 3 gouges, and slightly undercut the skirt in several places in front of the knees. The material would be stretched tightly over the rump, so scrape this smooth with the cabinet scraper, followed by gentle abrading with 320 grit garnet paper. To contrast with this smoothness, lightly hand tool the lower skirt material with a ⅛in (3mm) no. 8, no. 9 or no. 10 gouge, cutting shallow grooves around the shape of the legs.

Finishing

Inspect all the angles between adjacent surfaces, and the surfaces themselves, removing any deep cuts, nicks or other imperfections by paring and careful cutting by hand, using appropriately-sized no. 3 gouges and the skew chisel. Pare the edges of the base and the surface of the floor with a selection of no. 3 gouges until they are completely smooth and all pencil marks have been removed.

Fig 15.27 Use the nail to punch a tread on the soles and heels of the shoes, and cut the wrinkles of the stockings with the V tool.

Fig 15.28 Add tiny creases to the underside of the waistband and a button to the band itself.

Finally, smooth the skin of the face, arms, hands and legs by scraping with the ¼in (6mm) no. 3 gouge and the skew chisel. Use abrasives on a detailed carving of this sort sparingly, as the detail can easily be spoiled by over-enthusiastic rubbing.

Since lime is a rather bland and uninteresting wood, I applied Danish oil to bring out the colour, and allowed it to dry before polishing with a good quality colourless wax. If you have used another, more interesting wood, you could omit the oil and just use wax polish, although it will take several coats to bring the colour out fully. To complete the carving, glue a piece of felt to the base.

Glossary of Suitable Carving Woods

I have used all the woods listed here for carving. With the exception of cedar and yew, they are all hardwoods.

Acacia Hard and clean cutting; deep golden brown colour, darkening in time. Very pronounced grain pattern and very heavy. Suitable for abstract figures, as it finishes very smoothly; can also be used for detail, as its grain is tight. Less suitable for a portrait or a head, but ideal for birds, as its grain pattern gives an excellent feather effect.

Alder Bright orange when freshly cut, but fading to a pleasant pale ginger with freckles. Very light in weight and easy to carve. Large pieces are difficult to season without cracking, but small sections are suitable for miniature work and fine detail. Does not have a lot of grain pattern, but the flecking could detract from some carvings.

Almond Light brown to pink in colour; smooth and fine-grained; pleasant to work and good for detail. Fairly heavy with little grain pattern.

Apple Can be very slippery and hard; varies in colour from white to golden brown, often with streaks, and sometimes with contrast between the sapwood and heartwood. Frequently has curious arrow-like marks. Difficult to season without splitting, but its close and unpatterned grain makes it ideal for fine detail. Can often have a twist in it, making it difficult to cleave with an axe; a good wood for mallets.

Ash Pinkish-white in colour, but wax finish is blondish-silver; fairly hard and coarse-grained with pronounced hard and soft spots within the annual rings; logs have a good symmetrical marking. Suitable for less detailed carving; tends to attract dirt.

Beech Close-grained and heavy; pale brown with characteristic flecking and uniform pattern; can be incredibly hard. Suitable for utensils and items in contact with food, tool handles, bench tops, chair legs, etc. Will take detail.

Birch (Silver) Light and easy to carve with characteristic flecks and paper-like bark; prone to woodworm and rot. Fine close grain with little pattern, having a blondish-silver waxed finish; suitable for detail.

Box Creamy yellow colour; very close-grained and suitable for detail. Heavy and dense; sometimes used for tool handles. Not often available in large pieces, as it is very slow growing.

Cedar Medium hardness and texture, often with stringy patches, which need careful handling. Aromatic, which can become tiresome; medium brown colour with an even pattern. Fairly easy to work; will take detail and finishes well.

Cherry Various types, all suitable for all forms of carving. Some have considerable grain pattern; colours range from yellow to deep pink, sometimes with greenish-brown stripes running through. Some varieties are quick and easy to carve; others can be very hard.

Cherry Plum Light in colour and close-grained with little pattern; suitable for detail. Difficult to season because it tends to have a wind or twist in it.

Chestnut Coarse grain with plenty of pattern; pleasant brown colour, but turns yellow when wet. Not suitable for fine work or detail, but finishes well. Sometimes called the 'poor man's oak', as it looks similar, although it is not as hard or heavy.

Ebony Close-grained and deep brown to black in colour; uniform pattern; very dense and heavy. Suitable for tiny detailed carving. Usually only available in small pieces.

Elm Chocolate brown, with pronounced pattern and fairly coarse interlocked grain, making it difficult to carve. Lovely finished with wax polish, suitable for bold carving rather than fine detail.

Hawthorn Creamish-white and close-grained with uniform patterning; heavy and dense; clean cutting. Takes detail well.

Holly Heavy, dense and white; close-grained with very little pattern. Very smooth to work, being suitable for functional carvings, heads, etc. Difficult to find sound pieces of any significant size.

Holm oak Very heavy and hard; light brown in colour with characteristic oak patterning; usually straight-grained. Suitable for detail and takes a good polish. Ideal for carvings where weight is needed, such as book-ends, table lamps, etc.

Iroko Dark brown in colour; finishes with a nice sheen. Not easy to carve, as it has interlocked grain, but suitable for lettering outdoors, such as house name plates, since it resists the weather.

Laburnum Yellow sapwood and dark brown heartwood; close- and straight-grained with a fascinating pattern; crotches have particularly pretty patterning. Hard and heavy, but often rotten in the middle; cuts easily and cleanly. Will take detail, but rather too patterned for heads. Do not use in contact with food.

Laurel White with very little pattern; light in weight; takes detail well. Usually only available in small pieces.

Lime Very quick and easy to carve; pale brown in colour with uniform grain and not much pattern; boards sometimes have a bluish tinge. Suitable for all kinds of carving and often recommended for beginners, but rather bland. Prone to rot. Application of Danish oil will enhance its colour considerably.

Mahogany Many different types, ranging in colour from pale reddish-brown to dark chocolate; sometimes has interlocked grain. Various weights according to type, some close- and fine-grained; others very coarse. Can be useful for relief work, especially if you can fit the grain pattern into your design. Usually available in squared blocks.

Mulberry Deep yellow-brown, straight-grained with no particular pattern; hard and cuts cleanly. Takes detail well. Not easy to find.

Oak Many types, all varying in hardness, with a characteristic bold pattern. Can be very coarse-grained, also very smooth, tough, stringy and with fibrous soft areas. Not suitable for fine detail; better for large bold work, tooled carvings and functional carvings. The marked grain pattern can detract from the work if not placed carefully. Use brass fittings, not steel, as the latter will cause discolouration.

Pear Varies in colour from almost white to warm brown; close- and fairly straight-grained; can be very pretty. Easy to carve; finishes smoothly; suitable for detail as well as larger carvings.

Plane Heavy weight; light in colour with no marked pattern, but some cuts have flecks. Fairly coarse-textured with little variation in hardness; finishes well. Seasons quickly but can be very hard and slow to carve.

Plum A lovely wood with contrasting heartwood and sapwood; the former can vary from yellow-brown to deep red or purple. Has interesting grain patterns; cuts cleanly, with a pleasant smell; finishes well. Medium weight; fairly easy and quick to carve. Suitable for abstracts, but also takes detail. Usually only available in small pieces.

Poplar Rather stringy; pinkish-yellow colour; finishes well and takes a good polish. Fairly coarse, but will take detail. Easier to cut with a mallet and gouge than by hand.

Sycamore White, sometimes with streaks of green; often rippled grain with interesting patterns; sometimes quite bland; can be very hard. Straight-grained; will take detail and is ideal for reliefs; suitable for contact with food. Store vertically to prevent discolouration.

Rhododendron White when freshly cut, discolouring quickly to pale brown. Quick and easy to carve, with a very fine grain and little patterning. Takes detail well, but difficult to season without splitting.

Tree of heaven (Ailanthus) Coarse wood that finishes a silvery-white colour; marked pattern in the grain. Smells unpleasant when the bark is removed, but not noticeably when carved. Medium hardness; quite quick to work with mallet and gouge, but not by hand; not suitable for intricate detail.

Walnut Deep chocolate brown to purple heartwood and light brown sapwood; generally straight- and fairly close-grained with uniform patterning; can be very hard. Sapwood prone to woodworm. Suitable for all types of carving, but detail can become lost because of its dark colour.

Willow Light in colour, ranging from pinkish-yellow to white; stringy and coarse; can be woolly in texture, but is usually straight-grained and quite easy to carve. Difficult to season without cracking. More suited to large carvings; does not take detail well.

Yew A softwood with a delightful colour contrast of heartwood and sapwood; ranges in colour from pale sand to deep purple, particularly if dampened; fine-grained. Can be extremely difficult to carve; sometimes shatters when cut across the grain. Suitable for all types of carving, but avoid contact with food; sawdust can also be unpleasant.

Glossary of Terms

Angle chisel   See skew chisel.

Annual ring   Growth ring of a tree.

Arkansas stone   Natural sharpening stone found in the Ozark Mountains, USA.

Autumn wood   Darker edge of the annual ring found in trees growing in temperate zones; formed when the sap falls in late summer and autumn.

Back-bent gouge or chisel   Tool with blade curved backwards; used for cutting convex shapes in confined spaces.

Bark   Outer layer of a tree; protects the cambium (growing) layer.

Bench holdfast   Device to hold work flat on a work bench.

Bench hook   Device for steadying work while sawing.

Bench screw   Main screw that operates the vice fitted to a work bench.

Bench stone   Sharpening stone.

Bent-bladed   Gouge or chisel with a forward bend in the blade; useful for working inside concave shapes.

Bosting in, or out   Removing waste wood from, and general shaping of, a carving in the round before carving finer detail.

Bevel   Sloping surface immediately behind the cutting edge of a gouge or chisel.

Burnishing   Giving hardwood a shiny surface by rubbing it with a harder substance, or chips of the same wood.

Burr   Abnormal growth of wood. Also the rough edge left on the cutting edge of a tool after honing (sometimes referred to as a wire edge).

Cabinetmaker's scraper   Thin steel plate with sharpened edges for smoothing the wood surface.

Cambium layer   The growing layer of a tree.

Carver's chops   Swivelling, wooden-jawed vice mounted to the top of a bench.

Ceramic stone   Sharpening stone made from artificial sapphires, and used without a lubricant.

Checks   Surface cracks often visible in the ends of logs.

Chip carving   Using knife cuts to create a decorative pattern of triangular recesses.

Chisel   Cutting tool with bevelled, flat cutting edge.

Close-grained   Wood with closely-packed, narrow growth rings.

Coarse-grained   Wood with loosely-packed growth rings.

Combination stone   Sharpening stone with different grades of abrasive on each face.

Concave   Hollowed; outline or surface.

Convex   Rounded; outline or surface.

Corner chisel   See skew chisel.

Coping saw   Small-framed saw with narrow blade for cutting curves.

Cradle   Scrap wood fastened to bench to secure carving with the aid of wedges.

Cramp   (also known as a **clamp**) Device for clamping items together.

Cross grain   Wood in which the grain does not run lengthwise.

Deciduous   Tree that sheds its leaves after the annual growth period.

Dogleg chisel   A cranked tool with a double bend in the blade to offset the cutting edge.

Early wood   The portion of an annual ring that is formed first, characterized by larger pores (also known as spring wood).

Edge tool   Cutting tool sharpened on a stone (usually a hand tool).

End grain   Cross-sectional surface of wood, showing the pores.

Ferrule   Metal ring, usually brass, fixed around the lower end of a tool handle to prevent it from splitting.

Figure   Distinctive pattern on the surface of wood.

Fine-grained   See close-grained.

Fishtail gouge   Gouge with a cutting edge that widens out like a fish tail.

Flat gouge   A gouge with shallow curvature to the blade, such as a no. 3 (Swiss no. 2).

Fluter   Small, very deeply curved gouge.

Front-bent gouge or chisel   Tool with blade curved forwards; used for cutting concave shapes in confined spaces.

G-cramp   Form of clamping device with a G-shaped frame.

Garnet paper   Type of abrasive paper.

Gooseneck gouge   See front-bent gouge.

Gouge   Tool with cutting edge that is curved in cross-section.

Grain   The arrangement of the wood fibres.

Green wood   Newly cut, unseasoned wood.

Growth ring   See annual ring.

Grounding tool   Front-bent gouge or chisel.

Handcarving   Carving by hand pressure, without the use of a mallet.

Hard-grained   Wood with dense, hard grain.

Hardwood   Wood from broad-leaved trees with a more complex structure than softwood, sometimes known as porous wood; not necessarily very dense or hard wood.

Heart shake   Radial crack emanating from pith of the wood.

Heartwood   Inner wood of the tree; often darker in colour, harder, heavier and more durable than the sapwood.

Hollow grind   Slight hollowing of the bevel of a gouge, across its width, to improve cutting action by preventing the blade from acting as a wedge in the wood.

Honing   Sharpening on a stone.

Horns   The corners of the cutting edge of a gouge.

Hygroscopic   The ability of a material to absorb or release water.

Incised   Cut in below the surface of the wood.

India stone   Type of sharpening stone.

Interlocked grain   Repeated alternation of left- and right-hand spiral layers of growth in a tree, giving change in direction of grain.

In the round   Carving in three dimensions.

Kerf   Groove made by a saw cut.

Knife-edge slipstone   A slipstone with a very narrow edge to fit inside a V tool.

Knot   Part of a branch embedded in the trunk of a tree, or another branch.

Late wood   Part of the growth ring laid down after the early wood, often characterized by smaller, denser cells (also known as summer wood).

Leg   A short length of tree trunk or branch.

London Pattern   Standard type of carving gouge with a straight blade.

Macaroni tool   Edge tool with angular U-section.

Mallet   Striking tool for use with gouge or chisel.

Maquette   A preliminary model in clay or Plasticine, made before carving in wood.

Medullary rays   Radial vessels in the wood that allow transmission of sap; particularly visible in some coarse-grained hardwoods.

Multiform slipstone   A slipstone with a variety of shaped edges.

Needle leaf The spine-like leaf of a conifer or softwood tree.

Oilstone Sharpening stone used with oil as a lubricant.

Open-grained Wood with widely-spaced growth rings.

Parenchyma Thin-walled wood cells that store and transmit food within the tree (also known as soft tissue); may be radial or axial.

Paring gouge Long-bladed gouge with bevel on the inner surface of the cutting edge; not normally used in carving.

Parting tool Another name for a V tool; do not confuse with parting tool used in woodturning, which has another purpose.

Patina Gloss on a wood surface, produced by handling and age.

Phloem Inner bark of a tree.

Pierced carving A relief with parts of the background cut through completely.

Pith The central core of soft tissue in a tree trunk or branch.

Plane Tool with cutting iron, used for levelling and smoothing flat surfaces.

Polishing stone Used to produce a superior cutting edge after honing.

Pores The cross-section of vessels, seen clearly in coarse-grained woods.

Profile A drawing, or silhouette, of the outline of a figure.

Quick gouge A gouge with a deep sweep, or curve.

Quick-release vice A vice with a mechanism to disengage the screw thread, allowing the faceplate to be easily and quickly moved in or out.

Raising the grain Intentionally dampening the surface to make the wood fibres swell before abrading.

Raised lettering Letters carved in relief.

Rasp A file with individual cutting teeth.

Relief A carving that stands out above the background.

Riffler Type of small, curved rasp with a long handle.

Ring porous wood Hardwood with relatively large pores in its early wood, and small pores in its late wood.

Ring shakes Where layers of wood have separated longitudinally between the growth rings.

Roughing out Cutting away superfluous wood before carving.

Rot Decay due to fungi.

Sap The moisture circulating in a tree, containing nutrients.

Sapwood The outer part of a tree trunk that contains living cells; usually lighter in colour and softer than the heartwood.

Saw set Tool for setting the teeth angle of a saw.

Scraper See cabinetmaker's scraper.

Seasoning Allowing wood to dry after felling.

Setting out Marking the outline of a relief against the background.

Serifs The pointed ends of certain styles of letter.

Shakes Natural cracks that appear in wood as it dries.

Sharpening stone Man-made or natural abrasive stone on which a cutting edge is honed.

Short-grained Cross-grained wood in which the fibres fracture without splintering, tending to shatter and break easily under pressure.

Skew chisel A chisel with an acutely angled blade, usually bevelled on both sides, with a pointed cutting edge.

Slatestone Sharpening stone made from slate.

Slipstone Shaped stone to fit inside gouges and remove burr produced during honing.

Slurry Mixture of lubricant and metal particles produced during honing.

Softwood Wood from coniferous trees, lacking vessels and sometimes referred to as non-porous wood; does not necessarily apply to the softness of the wood – some softwoods are harder and denser than hardwoods.

Sole   The underside of a plane or spokeshave.

Spaded gouge   See fishtail gouge.

Spiral grain   Grain in which the fibres run in a spiral manner around and up the tree.

Spokeshave   Tool with an adjustable blade, which can be pushed or pulled with both hands to shape a carving; may have a flat or convex sole.

Spoonbit gouge   See front-bent gouge.

Spring wood   See early wood.

Star shakes   Several heart shakes, resembling a star in appearance.

Straight-grained   Wood in which the fibres lie parallel to its length.

Strop   Piece of leather used to wipe the cutting edge, following removal of the burr caused by honing.

Surform   Rasp-like tool for removing wood quickly.

Sweep   The curvature of a gouge blade.

Tang   The part of a tool blade that is inserted into the handle.

Temper   The correct hardness and resilience of a tool blade so that it will retain its cutting edge in use; achieved by heating the metal.

Texturing   Surface decoration of carving, sometimes to simulate hair, fur, feathers, etc.

Tooling   Patterning a surface with gouge cuts.

Tracheid   Long conducting cells, mostly of softwood tissue, that correspond to hardwood fibres; may also be present in some deciduous trees.

Undercut   Cutting under the edges of a relief design to lighten the carving or create shadow effect.

Uneven grain   Growth rings showing pronounced difference between early and late wood.

V tool   A tool with two cutting edges set at an angle to each other; used for cutting a V-shaped channel.

Veiner   Narrow, very deep gouge.

Vessels   Conductive, tube-like hardwood cells with open ends that lie end to end.

Vessel lines   Visible lines on longitudinal surfaces of heartwood with large-diameter vessels; produced by cutting lengthways across them.

Vice   For holding work securely to the work bench; has two faces brought together by a screw thread.

Vignette   A relief carving without a border.

Waterstone   Sharpening stone lubricated by water.

Washita   Type of sharpening stone.

Wheel dresser   Appliance used to re-surface a worn or glazed grinding stone.

Whittle   To shape wood by using knives only.

Wings   The two blades of a V tool.

Wire edge   See burr.

Xylem   Botanical term for wood.

Index

TITLES AVAILABLE FROM
GMC PUBLICATIONS

BOOKS

WOODTURNING

Adventures in Woodturning	*David Springett*		
Bert Marsh: Woodturner	*Bert Marsh*	Pleasure & Profit from Woodturning	*Reg Sherwin*
Bill Jones' Notes from the Turning Shop	*Bill Jones*	Practical Tips for Turners & Carvers	*GMC Publications*
Carving on Turning	*Chris Pye*	Practical Tips for Woodturners	*GMC Publications*
Colouring Techniques for Woodturners	*Jan Sanders*	Spindle Turning	*GMC Publications*
Decorative Techniques for Woodturners	*Hilary Bowen*	Turning Miniatures in Wood	*John Sainsbury*
Faceplate Turning: Features, Projects, Practice	*GMC Publications*	Turning Wooden Toys	*Terry Lawrence*
Green Woodwork	*Mike Abbott*	Useful Woodturning Projects	*GMC Publications*
Illustrated Woodturning Techniques	*John Hunnex*	Woodturning: A Foundation Course	*Keith Rowley*
Keith Rowley's Woodturning Projects	*Keith Rowley*	Woodturning Jewellery	*Hilary Bowen*
Make Money from Woodturning	*Ann & Bob Phillips*	Woodturning Masterclass	*Tony Boase*
Multi-Centre Woodturning	*Ray Hopper*	Woodturning: A Source Book of Shapes	*John Hunnex*

WOODCARVING

The Art of the Woodcarver	*GMC Publications*	Wildfowl Carving Volume 1	*Jim Pearce*
Carving Birds & Beasts	*GMC Publications*	Wildfowl Carving Volume 2	*Jim Pearce*
Carving Realistic Birds	*David Tippey*	Woodcarving: A Complete Course	*Ron Butterfield*
Carving on Turning	*Chris Pye*	Woodcarving for Beginners: Projects,	
Decorative Woodcarving	*Jeremy Williams*	Techniques & Tools	*GMC Publications*
Practical Tips for Turners & Carvers	*GMC Publications*	Woodcarving Tools, Materials & Equipment	*Chris Pye*

PLANS, PROJECTS, TOOLS & THE WORKSHOP

40 More Woodworking Plans & Projects	*GMC Publications*	Sharpening: The Complete Guide	*Jim Kingshott*
Electric Woodwork: Power Tool Woodworking	*Jeremy Broun*	Sharpening Pocket Reference Book	*Jim Kingshott*
The Incredible Router	*Jeremy Broun*	Woodworking Plans & Projects	*GMC Publications*
Making & Modifying Woodworking Tools	*Jim Kingshott*	The Workshop	*Jim Kingshott*

TOYS & MINIATURES

Designing & Making Wooden Toys	*Terry Kelly*	Making Wooden Toys & Games	*Jeff & Jennie Loader*
Heraldic Miniature Knights	*Peter Greenhill*	Miniature Needlepoint Carpets	*Janet Granger*
Making Board, Peg & Dice Games	*Jeff & Jennie Loader*	Restoring Rocking Horses	*Clive Green & Anthony Dew*
Making Little Boxes from Wood	*John Bennett*	Turning Miniatures in Wood	*John Sainsbury*
Making Unusual Miniatures	*Graham Spalding*	Turning Wooden Toys	*Terry Lawrence*

CREATIVE CRAFTS

The Complete Pyrography	*Stephen Poole*	Making Knitwear Fit	*Pat Ashforth & Steve Plummer*
Creating Knitwear Designs	*Pat Ashforth & Steve Plummer*	Miniature Needlepoint Carpets	*Janet Granger*
Cross Stitch on Colour	*Sheena Rogers*	Tatting Collage	*Lindsay Rogers*
Embroidery Tips & Hints	*Harold Hayes*		